RED IVY, GREEN EARTH MOTHER

RED IVY, GREEN EARTH MOTHER

Ai Bei

Translated by Howard Goldblatt

PEREGRINE SMITH BOOKS
SALT LAKE CITY

First edition
92 91 90   5 4 3 2 1

This is a Peregrine Smith Book, published by
Gibbs Smith, Publisher
P.O. Box 667
Layton, Utah 84041

Design by Randall Smith
Cover illustration © 1990 by Chu Ko
Printed and bound in the United States of America

Library of Congress Cataloging-in-Publication Data

Ai, Bei.
   Red ivy , green earth mother / Ai Bei :
   [translated from the Chinese by Howard
   Goldblatt].
   p. cm.
   ISBN 0-87905-292-9
   1. Ai, Bei—Translations, English. I. Goldblatt, Howard, 1939- . II. Title.
   PL2833.5.E45R44   1990
   895.1'352—dc20   90-33849
                                     CIP

CONTENTS

FOREWORD

Amy Tan

I N 1989, I WAS INVITED TO SPEAK AT THE WRITERS AT Work Conference held in Park City, Utah. I was to be on a panel with a Chinese writer named Ai Bei, a critically acclaimed short story writer who was visiting from Beijing.

Since I could not write in Chinese, and Ai Bei could not write in English, we communicated prior to the conference via translated letters. We agreed that our topic would be open: Ai Bei would discuss the current situation in Chinese literature; I would offer supporting comments on the migration of Chinese literature to America.

A few more translated communications later, we decided to title our panel discussion, "The Uncertain Path," referring to the artistic dilemmas facing Chinese writers, and perhaps also reflecting our uncertainty as to what two writers from different worlds could possibly talk about in common. Little did we know how much our title could describe the crisis that so many Chinese people would later face—and Ai Bei would be one of them.

Several months went by before we finally met at Sundance, Utah, to do a special reading prior to the conference itself. It was June 10, 1989, less than a week after the tumultuous events at Tiananmen Square.

I think anyone would be struck in meeting Ai Bei for the first time. She communicates an immediate presence without the need of translators. She's vibrant, observant. She instantly comes across as having a "strong character," and by that I mean interesting in the Chinese sense, and not offensive in the American sense. She has strong opinions about nearly everything, but she is not opinionated; she is willing to listen. When we met, she shook my hand with a firm grip.

I stammered out a few awkward Chinese phrases, apologizing for my bad pronunciation. We found out our mothers both came from Shanghai. It was a nice social chat, but I was frustrated that I could not ask her what was really on my mind: "What do you really think about the situation in China?"

"Situation" is the safe word to use with Chinese people you don't know, when you don't know their political or personal obligations to China. At the time even I had personal reasons to be reserved in what I said on the subject of the "massacre," as it was called in American newspapers, or the "turmoil," as they referred to it in China. Many of my family members, including one of my sisters, were living in Beijing and were affiliated with either the government or the university. During the month of June everyone who had family or friends in China agonized over whether to write, whether to call, whether it was more prudent not to say anything lest it damaged your family's "situation" in China.

So I wondered what Ai Bei was thinking, whether she had these same concerns—about not saying too much because of family and friends in China, about being cautious because of possible repercussions to her professional standing as a writer in China. I also knew at the time that most writers in China are selected and nurtured by the government, are paid a monthly wage, and see their books get into print, thanks to the government's various publishing arms. I had been told that Ai Bei was attached to a military unit; in what way, I didn't know. So I thought perhaps she would acknowledge the tragedy, but remain reserved in giving any further opinions. After all, I had met other Chinese writers recently whose opinions seemed shaped by something other than their own self-search.

"We can write anything we want," one of these other writers had said. "Any theme, any subject, no restrictions, no censorship." Her hearty claim and the incredulous looks of her American audience gave me the sensation of a pin being traced against the surface of a balloon.

"This is very encouraging to hear," said someone from the audience. "And what about homosexual literature in China? In America, we still have problems—certain works don't get funded, can't get published. Do you have a similar problem in China?" The question was translated.

"We have no such problem in China," the writer answered confidently. The audience sighed, smiled.

"Who are your homosexual writers then? What do they write about?" A pause as the question was translated.

"We have no homosexual literature in China," explained the writer. "Because we do not have this problem—homosexuality. It does not exist."

I believed that the writer was giving an honest answer. She believed what she was saying, no matter how sanitized—or rather, anesthetized—it came across to her American audience. And that to me was truly sad, to not even know what truths she held in her hand. Truth is the greatest tool a fiction writer has. That's what makes fiction so believable.

Now I should relay what happened when Ai Bei gave a talk to her American audience—and why I believe she is different from other writers I have met from China.

That day in June she stood in front of an audience of fifty or so writers and filmmakers. As she was being introduced in English, she looked agitated, on edge. And then she sprang up, walked to the front and started to talk.

Her voice was not wistful or sad—it was outright angry, bitter, anguished and filled with self-reproach for watching this nightmare in China from a safe place. She wished her blood could have spilled on the streets along with that of the students. Her talk was delivered in Chinese, and painstakingly translated, sentence by sentence. But you could understand her meaning by simply listening to her voice, the purity of the emotion. We were pushing back tears at the end of her short talk.

And then Phyllis Barber, one of the conference coordinators, read an excerpt from Ai Bei's short story, "Bala's Dream." In that story, I could hear the same voice that had filled the speech just moments before. That is what I often look for in another writer's work—the connection between the writer's actual voice and that which is found in his or her stories.

Over the next week, I gradually overcame my shyness and shame of speaking to Ai Bei in my childish version of Mandarin. Every day she encouraged me, "Amy Tan, your Chinese is getting better, really, much, much better." And so we talked—about other writers, food, China, my family, photography, Chinese and American jokes, Chinese and American manners—and then the horror of watching the news on television, of people who were about to be executed, of people whose own sisters and friends were turning them in. We found we were similar in our thoughts on so many things. She called me "Mei-mei," little sister, half in jest, half in friendship (I am older than Ai Bei).

And then she talked about her own future as a writer, as a Chinese citizen. "Amy Tan," she said, "what would you do?" And it made me realize a major difference between us. I would never have to really face the questions she was now asking herself.

On the day of our panel discussion, Ai Bei entered the room and I could see she was shaking. The room was filled to capacity, but I sensed it was not the crowd that made her nervous. She quietly told me what had happened just minutes before. She had received a call from her military unit in Beijing. They admonished her for speaking out on Voice of America, for giving interviews on her views of the Tiananmen Square turmoil. They ordered her to return home immediately. She refused, and instantly cast herself into the role of exile—cut off from her motherland, her family, friends, and the professional prestige she had established for herself in China as a writer. That afternoon, she gave a speech about literature. She spoke about literature as if her life depended on it, nothing held back.

I've chosen to relate these personal anecdotes because they are relevant to what I think and feel about Ai Bei's fiction. I also included them because too often translated fiction comes across the ocean as having been written by faceless people with names that are too difficult to pronounce (hers is pronounced somewhat like "eye bay"). And certainly there has been the problem of getting American readers hooked on any story in which characters call each other "comrade" and dwell on problems and deprivations we can't begin to comprehend as anything except overly dramatic.

Let me warn the reader. In Ai Bei's stories, you won't find any tales with happy endings, no easy reconciliation with the world. In fact, I would guess that her stories are not what either Chinese or American audiences would consider "easy reading." There are no stories about the mild malaise of middle-classdom, boring marriages, uncomfortable family reunions, dead-end lifestyles and the like. The so-called themes and style contain none of the spare, carefully controlled or understated traits that this country's reviewers prize so much in current literature—the drop-dead scene and the narrator's non-reaction to it.

I also think reviewers would be hard-pressed to describe Ai Bei's fiction as resembling any kind of style, school of literature, or genre. To be sure, her fiction concerns life in a dirty realism sort of way—at times. But then there are the dark surrealistic images of the mind, providing counterpart to daily existence.

And her fiction is certainly suffused with the most lush, sensual and sexual prose I have seen coming out of recent China. But I would say this is merely one quality of her voice, not the dominating aspect of her themes. And certainly there are moments—dialogue and images—punctuated with sharp humor and wry observations.

If you pushed me to the wall and forced me to say which American writer I thought Ai Bei's literary voice most resembled, I would have to say Allen Ginsberg—but only in the tone of her voice. In Ai Bei's stories, you get an immediate sense of her "presence," a strong and distinctive voice. Her voice has an edge to it. The anger is explosive. She gnaws on the anguish. She writes stories, as if her life depended on it.

And in fact, that is what her three stories and one novella are about: difficult issues about existence—the self in conflict with both society and the self that society has created. From the very first sentence of "Bala's Dream," you sense the narrator's disgust at the moral decay that arises from self-ambitions—a husband who fakes love for an old Swedish woman to secure his future, a beggar who fakes an oozing sore for charity, and the narrator herself who has faked a righteous moral good when it was really her ego at stake. And so the narrator goes off for a pilgrimage to mythical places of innocence, beauty, and pure passion—perhaps to purge herself, perhaps to destroy the last of her illusions. She shows off a tough exterior, a street-smart savvy about the ways of the world and its façade. And—just as she suspected—the mythical places have turned into tourist traps, film locations, and clichéd artist retreats. She presses on, walking with her guide. She reaches the primitive village of Bala's Dream—and the unexpected happens, something that leaves her vulnerable again.

I won't tell you the ending, only say that it raises the question: Will the dream you think can save you ultimately destroy you in the end?

The other stories in *Red Ivy, Green Earth Mother* are just as rich, just as powerful. It is the self in conflict with the world. The stories raise questions about the odds for or against existence and survival of the individual.

In looking at any translated work, it's always difficult to provide any casual comparison or critique of style or theme, technique or literary intent. Even with the best of translations,

the author's voice, words, and rhythms change—necessarily so
to make it accessible to readers of another culture. So much
can be lost in translation. So much can be excised by wary
editors on both shores. In fact, I have often wondered in
reading current literature arriving from the PRC, "How much
has been left out?"

This anthology represents a possible first: fiction by a
Chinese writer that is published in this country in its entirety
—unexpurgated, uncensored. In fact, I am told that some of
these stories, which were published in literary magazines in
Beijing, had been edited extensively; politically or sexually
provocative passages were trimmed out. Ai Bei has chosen to
restore her stories to the original.

And, happily for Ai Bei and readers alike, she was able to
work with Howard Goldblatt, one of the best translators of
Chinese literature in the Western world. My personal library
contains many books translated by Mr. Goldblatt—from revo-
lutionary literature of the 1930s to the latest books allowed to
"emigrate" from the PRC. He has both a Chinese ear and a
literary one.

In translating fiction, oftentimes certain colloquial expres-
sions and culture-specific references are changed for the sake of
clarity and fluidity of the story. This is also the case with Ai
Bei's work. But how I wish some of those lines could have
stayed! In Chinese, they convey witticisms, puns, rich images
and historical allusions. I tried some of them on friends of
mine, the litmus test being this: If they laughed or said "ahh,"
the phrase should have stayed as written in the colloquial
Chinese; if they said, "huh?" the phrase was changed for appro-
priate reasons. My brief, uncontrolled study only showed that
Howard Goldblatt was right. But you should know, there is
another rich dimension to Ai Bei's fiction that you won't know
unless you are able to hear and understand her stories in
Chinese.

Even with that, I think you will find the power and passion
and truth in Ai Bei's stories. Her voice demands to be heard,
deserves to be listened to. These are the first of her stories to
be "told" in English. And I am sure there will be many more,
about difficult lives in China—or perhaps about a new life in
America. I think we are fortunate to have her voice join and
enrich our literature, our thinking about the world.

BALA'S DREAM

I F MY HUSBAND HADN'T FALLEN IN LOVE WITH THAT haggle-toothed old Swedish woman, if Father hadn't remarried during the hundred-day mourning period for Mother, if two-year-old Yuanyuan hadn't wiggled her fanny and screeched into the microphone, if Younger Sister hadn't faked a divorce to get into college, if my elder cousin hadn't slept with a black man for the twenty-six-dollar TOEFL registration fee, if my brother-in-law hadn't cooked a spicy meal every Saturday for the French expert on *Dream of the Red Chamber* so he could study the novel with him, if Uncle Liu, who'd participated in the Long March, hadn't suffered a stroke because his grandson's illicit business had been shut down, if I hadn't learned of the argument over wages between the two Buddhist nuns, driving one mad and the other to suicide, if half the newspaper and TV reports were true, if the charity out of which I'd given the crippled beggar two yuan were really part of my nature, and the beggar hadn't actually wrapped his good leg with gauze to make it look crippled, if I hadn't denounced my advisor's position during the defense of my master's thesis in a hall packed with experts and professors just to make a name for myself and further my ambitions, if I hadn't exploited my chastity in dealing with men, if there weren't an international AIDS epidemic, if Iraq and Iran weren't engaged in a protracted war, if my slashed artery hadn't been sutured in time, then I definitely wouldn't have been riding in this rickety old Jeep for two days and nights, oozing pus from my eyes and nose! Car sickness is worse than leisurely despair.

This is Xishuang Banna. What'll it be, a hotel or a hostel?

Yan Lun, my driver, asked about arrangements out of
habit. His presumption angered me. What makes you think
I want to stay here?

Everybody who comes here stays a few days.

Not me.

The pigheaded Yan Lun stopped the Jeep anyway. He got
out, but I ignored him and stayed put.

You can get out and take a look around without having to
stay.

Since he'd softened his tone, I saved him embarrassment
by getting out to take a look around. What I saw disappoint-
ed me. A far-off Xishuang Banna, shrouded in mystery, had
lived in my mind since I was a little girl, but I'd never thought
I'd actually see it. Now I was going on thirty, and here it was,
as ordinary and gloomy a place as any farming village in
Henan or Anhui. Village girls as lovely as a song, banana
plantations, coconut groves, and quaint bamboo huts I'd
expected to see were all withered and neglected. What a pity,
I muttered. This is Xishuang Banna?

Don't be ridiculous! The place you saw in the movies was
actually in Yunnan at the Greater Menglun Botanical Garden,
the Lesser Mengyang Primeval Forest, Ruili, and Wanding. I
was the driver when they shot those scenes.

Maybe people immortalized it, then went and destroyed it.
I'd rather say I never came to Xishuang Banna.

That's stupid! You're standing on Banna soil under a
Banna sky.

Yan Lun took his anger out on the Jeep door as he jumped
in and slammed it shut, then started the engine. We drove
for a while, until I figured we'd left Xishuang Banna far
behind us, then turned and looked out the window. Clusters
of green hedge bamboo spewed out of the fiery red earth like
emerald fountains, prompting a bewildering question: How
could earth so red spew "fountains" so green? The more I
thought about it, the more puzzled I became; it was like
trying to comprehend the meaning of life.

Hey, little friend, want a hedgehog?

The little boy was clearly interested, but he just stood

there, school bag over his back, looking puzzled and frightened.

I bought it in the suburbs yesterday for my advisor's grandson. But he's so young he nearly killed it. Take it. It eats eggs, I just fed it . . .

My gestures and expression were purer than the angels, I'm sure of that, and the boy was touched; so was a passerby. I could vaguely sense something large and white looming beneath the twisted date tree behind me, and although I couldn't see his face, something inside me told me it was a man. An air of gloom surrounded me, very tantalizing.

If you get tired of playing with it, set it free in the wooded area of the park. Don't just let it go out on the road or give it to anybody younger than you . . . I paused, sensing that to go on would be an act, possibly for the benefit of the person behind me. All I had to do, I felt, was turn around to be rewarded for my actions by an expression of gratitude. But the stronger the temptation to turn around, the greater the force that kept me looking straight ahead.

Thanks, Auntie!

Bye-bye!

I climbed into the Jeep with a sense of missed opportunity, but then a breeze came to my rescue. My straw hat blew off my head and landed at my feet. He picked it up and handed it to me, and our eyes met. Gazes of longing passed between us, but we quickly hid behind polite smiles, as though there were nothing left to be said. We drove off.

Just where do you want to go?

Yan Lun's voice was filled with emotion as he brought the Jeep to a screeching halt, throwing me violently forward, then hurling me back against the seat, which I grabbed tightly. When he leaned up against the steering wheel, I could see the muscles of his back ripple. I wanted to reach out and rub his back, but I couldn't do that. At some point in our trip, he'd stopped being formal around me, and that's when he'd begun swearing and bitching about things I couldn't figure out. I'd kept a stern look on my face from the very beginning, so there'd be no doubt about the distance between us. Now that we'd stopped, I was more carsick than ever, but since I had nothing left to throw up, my stomach just churned as I was wracked by dry heaves.

I don't know what's gotten into people like you over the past few years, why you all want to come here. It disgusts me to have to drive you female reporters, artists, and singers around! It's always goddamn something: you spot some goddamn flower or some goddamn tree, and you want me to stop the car so you can have your goddamn picture taken with your arm around me or cuddling up with a big smile, all hot and bothered, like I don't have the guts to do anything. Shit!

He said Shit! with style, like a manifesto for humiliated men everywhere, or as if he were giving me a warning. I ignored it, preferring to luxuriate in his bitching.

Some woman from the Far East Song and Dance Troupe put on a show at Cat's Ear Cave once, and since she didn't have anything to do after dinner, she insisted I take her into the woods to gather wildflowers. It was so foggy that a member of a film crew damn near shot me for a deer! The muscles in his back rippled more tantalizingly than ever when he was mad. Just where do you want to go?

Anywhere, the farthest, most-deserted place there is.

And where's that supposed to be?

Anywhere.

Okay, I'll take you to a hidden village in a valley of the great snow-capped mountain, Bala's Dream, so remote even the spirits don't know its name. I'll feed you to the bears!

Thank you.

He snapped his head around ferociously and gave me a look that felt as if he'd ripped a chunk of flesh off my body. I could barely stand it. Then he laughed and jammed his foot down on the gas pedal. The rear end of the rickety old Jeep shuddered a couple of times, then we started forward with fits and jerks. The fog got thicker and thicker, until the mountain road seemed to break up and disappear. The way the front tires were always on the verge of rolling off the edge of a cliff scared the wits out of me.

An old fellow came here a couple of years back to study the butterfly orchids at the base of Bala's Dream and got lost. He didn't return to camp for several days, and I was the one who carried his body out of that fucking village.

He glanced at me in the mirror, looking very smug, but I kept a deadpan expression on my face to deny him the satisfaction of frightening me. So he stomped down on the gas pedal and drove as close to the edge of the cliff as possible, until it seemed that the tires were riding on air. I was scared to death. The smell of gasoline made me feel like throwing up, and my poor stomach was twisted up in painful knots. I wanted to take a Dramamine, but the Jeep was bumping around so badly I couldn't pour the water, and I refused to ask him to stop. When I looked in the mirror, I saw a drowning infant, ghostly pale and worn out, the lifeless eyes betraying the fear and misery in her heart. God, I hated that look, but what frightened me more was the essence of weakness it revealed. I quickly turned and looked out the window, where I saw a huge, gorgeous sun following our Jeep over the tips of deep green trees. When I got tired of looking at the sun, I took off my jacket and put it over my head so I could bask in the warmth of the sun's rays. The pattern of the jacket transformed the sun into a resplendent, fleshy kaleidoscope of colors. I enjoyed the fantasy of holding it in my hand. The Jeep screeched to a halt.

That's what you call slash-and-burn cultivation, he shouted. Get out and take a picture, go on.

Yan Lun's shout jerked me out of the colors of the sun and back to the real world. I climbed out of the Jeep, ignoring the look of ridicule on his face. The side of the hill across from us was scarred and blackened, but the mountain rising above it was covered with a blanket of greens of every shape and hue.

Up there, that's a primeval forest.

I looked up at the mountain, which was covered with puny shrubs as crooked as dogs' legs, hardly worthy of the grand term primeval forest. I'd once had the thrill of being in a primeval forest in the Great Xing'an Mountains of Heilongjiang, where the canopy of intertwined branches blocks out the sun and sky and forms a vast world of shadows. Not a blade of grass or a single flower in that shadowy world, and

5

no human figures in sight, although from time to time you can hear the screech of a wild animal or the cry of a bird. The heavy, damp carpet of fallen leaves, at least six inches thick, muffles your steps until you're transported into a world of dreams. Mounds of ancient roots, living in the past, present, and future, call to you like doddering old men to rest in the crooks of their backs. Many of the old trees remain standing long after they've died and begun to decay, dissolving into a cloud of dust at the slightest touch. Some are already as much earth as they are tree, their corruption fertilizing the lush green saplings nearby. Tens of thousands of old trees, whose identical branches point to heaven and brush the ground, absorb the essence of sky and earth and the spirit of all living things, to live and perish, year after year, generation upon generation. Darkness and light interplay in the rain and mist like the sorrows of an iron man crying secretly in the boundless, serene depths.

The overwhelming solitude and unfathomable antiquity seemed to put me in touch with a colossal understanding, achieved in one glorious instant. At dusk I embraced the damp trunk of a tree so tightly that my heart and the tree's age rings seemed to beat in harmony; the fatigue of a long, long journey and years of cherished desires were all validated at that moment. I cried, the hot tears streaming into my feeble heart. Could it be that the placenta that had nurtured me in the womb was buried in this soil? Why else would I have had the feeling of coming home after so long? I was lost; maybe the forest wanted to take me back into its bosom. Yet I was surprisingly unafraid as I walked on aimlessly. I emerged from the forest as dawn broke, where the morning sun shone down on my face, like any other day. When my companion found me, she said I looked like a different person.

My shadow huddled coyly at my feet, like a little turtle, under the noonday sun. This was probably the only time of day you could enjoy such a relaxing ride on the number 104 streetcar. We pulled up at the Temple of Earth, announced by the conductor as if we'd landed in hell. I spotted him as I was getting off. We were both delighted, yet our looks of surprise betrayed expectations that would have astonished us. But that didn't stop him from boarding the streetcar, or me from getting off. God, I hated that sort of deceptive self-respect, so I turned and went back to my seat. His eyes lit up as he rushed over to the empty seat beside me like a guard dog; in the calm moment that followed, I became immediately conscious of a familiar, yet slightly unsettling smell of books. He looked at me with the naked innocence of a newborn infant, the innocence I yearned for.

You're really tan. Like a father's greeting at a train station.

Just got back. The primeval forest in the Great Xing'an Mountains is incredibly mystical! I said excitedly.

Are you a northerner who grew up in the south? He looked at me long and hard, as though he already knew the answer.

Uh-huh. I like southerners for their calculated richness of emotion, but then I like the openness and simple honesty of northerners. It's probably impossible to find someone with all those qualities. It's my strong emotional needs that make me so miserable all the time. Sometimes I feel like a rice shoot that's been planted on a mountaintop, and sooner or later I'll wither and die there. I paused to look out the window so he couldn't see the forlorn look on my face. Opening up like that to someone I hardly knew embarrassed me.

Emotionalism always causes pain. But it's worse if you don't know how to control your emotions. Like he was reading it out of a book.

His understanding caused the leaves of my life to flutter in the wind. We sat in silence as the streetcar traveled from one end of its route to the other. When I'm down in the dumps, I'd rather be abandoned by everyone in the world than have to listen to the sweet talk of any man.

Are you going to take a picture? Yan Lun held out an automatic camera.

I don't like the soil here. It nurtures itself until its face is red and lustrous, but everything that grows out of it is emaciated.

7

Look at those tall mountains; they grew out of this soil, didn't they?

The distant mountain peaks were bathed in the blood red rays of the setting sun, and in the valley between the two nearby mountains, a line of towering evergreens stood side by side, their branches intertwined, their bone white roots covering the ground beneath the vast, shadowy canopy like a gloomy curtain, giving an observer the feeling that a savage act was about to occur behind them. Just as I was about to marvel aloud at the sight, I noticed that Yan Lun was waiting to see what my reaction would be, and my excitement vanished, replaced by the look of indifference I so frequently and naturally affected. I scrutinized his face, not letting any expression slip past my eyes. He seemed uneasy: his uneven eyebrows, bushy in places, scraggly in others, were twisted, his thick, upturned lips were twitching like silkworms. Managing to hold back his complaints, he said impatiently:

People come here to stare at local girls bathing in the canal and the Wa women who give birth in the water, that and the rare evergreens . . . they all take pictures. How about you?

Suddenly I felt that he and I had been born under different moons, that his world didn't belong to me and that he'd have trouble entering mine. Year after year of driving for us so-called big-city, cultured folk, with all he'd seen and heard, had given him a superficial understanding with which he was measuring and trying to entrap me. I felt like laughing in his face, but all those years of upbringing, manners, education and degrees had driven the talent of carefree laughter out of me. My husband said I couldn't laugh if I was tickled under the arm. All those powerful forces had ground me into dust, then reconstituted me in their image.

We came down from the mountain and ate lunch in a town called Purple Lady. Since it was market day, the tiny square was packed with little old ladies, little old men, little peaches, little tomatoes, and little onions. A man was holding up some caterpillars, proclaiming them to be the secret ingredient for a nostrum used in the Imperial Palace, and someone else was using a trained monkey as an enticement to buy his bogus rat poison. The place was like a pot of boiling gruel, a chaotic,

8

steamy mess, with flies, mosquitoes, and the stench of pig shit and goat piss; it was a tumultuous scene of people scurrying back and forth rubbing elbows and brushing up against each other's backs. Strolling in this little town, with its frightening array of ghostly airs and flying pests, clouded your eyes as a reminder that you were a wild horse, not a human being. Fighting off the nausea of flies swarming around me, I forced down a couple of mouthfuls of sticky rice alongside an outdoor brazier, while Yan Lun went into a little shop to buy some cigarettes, staying in there so long I began to wonder what he was up to. With anger in my heart, I used the most abusive language I knew to get him to leave. But instead of reacting angrily, he merely grinned foolishly and gave me a look of such unfathomable mystery I was bewildered.

Our Jeep finally pulled up at the foot of snow-capped Bala's Dream after negotiating a wildly twisting, bumpy road that nearly cost me the nine lives I'd been given. My feet were so swollen I couldn't get out of the Jeep, and the pains in my chin and chest were so unbearable I didn't dare take a deep breath. Yan Lun hadn't uttered a word all morning, nor had he so much as glanced at me in the mirror. After bringing the Jeep to a stop, he slowly opened the door and helped me out. His hands seemed cold to me, and shaky.

If we drive any more, the Jeep'll fall apart. His voice seemed far away and sluggish. So after covering the Jeep with a plastic tarp, he picked up our bags and started walking toward a row of thatched huts. Since my feet wouldn't do my bidding, I leaned against a tree. He turned impatiently and came back to help me walk by holding my arm. But before we'd taken two steps, I pushed his arm away roughly, gritted my teeth, and walked under my own power. I figured that if I kept moving along, one mechanical step after another, I could probably keep it up until I dropped dead. He glanced at me with a respectful glint in his eyes, letting me move under my own power, and as we drew near to the row of huts, I asked him:

Is this Bala village? Didn't you say it was on the other side of the snow-capped mountain?

Right, it'll take us two days to get there! My exhaustion

and frustrations returned with a rush; he was waiting gleefully for the look of horror he knew his comment would produce.

Two days? I was stunned, but I tried not to show it. It's still light, I said, so why aren't we starting out?

Now it was his turn to be stunned. His thick, silkwormlike lips twitched briefly as he flipped his bag over his shoulder and made as if to start walking, to frighten me. We can't drive. Can you walk?

I don't know if I was tired or being masochistic, but I looked at him and asked derisively, Can you?

Ignoring me, he turned savagely and headed off toward the obscure little path that led to snow-capped Bala's Dream. With no time for regrets, I followed him. Would this be the trek that crippled me? Would I reach my destination alive? No way to tell, but he'd make it, that I knew. His thick purple lips, the rippling muscles on his back, and the shoulders as broad and strong as those of a horse were proof that he'd easily outlast me. With him around I knew I could torment myself as much as I wanted without fear. But this only showed how emotionally dependent I was, and I hated that. From the first realization that I was a girl others tended to like, I had invariably demanded the love of people I loved. With it I was as contented as a flower in full bloom; without it my tears flowed like autumn rains.

My first unhappy love affair had involved a boy who declared he couldn't live a day without me. But the depth of my feelings so unnerved him that he fled in panic from a love that blanketed the earth and blotted out the sky straight into the arms of another woman with whom he could live in peace. My scorched heart was still smoldering when I came to the realization that if you wanted someone, to receive that love was bliss, to lose it sheer torture. I remember writing in my diary once: Love is my cruelest enemy, the only one with the power to torture me to within an inch of my life. Anyone who longs for someone else's affections is like a lamb waiting meekly on a sacrificial altar. Father asked me after this, Can you live without your need for love? No, I said, I have to be able to accept love or reject it. I have to be able to enjoy it when it comes and calmly give it up when it goes. People are funny—they always seek and demand those very things the world cannot supply. Father laughed and said, In the process of losing her first love, my daughter has gained wisdom. And yet I hate it, this wisdom that's beyond my ability to put it into practice. After years of being battered by love, which has left me exhausted and worn out, I still want to love and be loved, even though it's brought me nothing but self-loathing and disgust, even a desire to bring this confused life to an early end. Self-contempt is probably the worst trick life can play on you.

Ten members of our graduate class boarded a motorboat belonging to the South China Sea Fleet for a field trip to study the cultures of people in the South China Sea. We departed from the port of Sanya and sailed for two days and nights. Since I was seasick, I stayed below decks, not daring to show my face outside. But my girlfriend dragged me out on deck at sunset on the second day, when the sea was particularly calm. Warm autumn winds and the hazy surface of the sea stretching as far as the eye could see produced a strange feeling that I could spend the rest of my life on this boat without ever seeing land again. We were only a tiny speck on a vast blue-gray sea, just waiting to be swallowed up by the first ferocious wave or strong wind. I glanced at my traveling companions—the captain, the sailors, the graduate students and their instructors—discovering that class and station had been obliterated in our boundless solitude, and that we were all alike, all equal. A gull flew overhead, way up in the sky, so high we couldn't hear the tale it was telling, and could only see the interminable flapping of its wings. Where could it land to rest? Was there a tiny island somewhere, some scrawny tree? My heart tightened, struck by a palpable desperation so enormous and sinister that it seemed to crumble in the silent grip. I shivered, even though it wasn't cold, and yearned desperately to see him. He'd been sitting at the stern since that morning, just gazing out at the sea.

The sea made me feel like a child who's lost its mother's breast. I sat down beside him, and was immediately caught up in his melancholic mood. Gradually my heart settled down. He was like a broad riverbed that could calm the raging waters flowing above it.

Women are like ancient junks in constant search of a safe haven. Give me a look of tenderness, he said calmly as his arm slid naturally around my shoulders. I had found my haven, a sweet, tranquil refuge at dawn. Maybe only a man could supply the primary ingredients of my life; maybe only a man could make me whole. Maybe the distinguishing trait of women all over the world is their inability to be emotionally independent. He held my hand in his, bringing a welcome calmness to my emotions. I was like an infant lying in a cradle suffused with the intoxicating fragrance of mother's milk. I gazed up into his placid eyes. Just then his thesis adviser, old Ben Xiang, appeared at the stern, talking to himself. He stirred and drew his hand back, then moved imperceptibly away from me. All this took only a fraction of a second, and he wasn't even aware of it. Nor, it seemed, was Professor Ben Xiang, who appeared blissfully unaware of the lightning-quick changes that had occurred between us. Feeling better? he asked kindly.

I felt abandoned, insulted, abused. But I didn't say anything, even though I was nearly in tears.

Much better. I gave her one of those extra-strength seasick pills my wife sent along, and she's much better. He spat out the words "my wife" clumsily. I looked away so they couldn't see the look of disgust on my face. His inability to control his common side embarrassed him and made him uneasy. But Professor Ben Xiang just nodded to show how relieved he was, then walked off talking to himself.

We didn't say anything to each other, nor did we move closer together as we sat there in silence until nightfall. As I got up to leave, he grasped my cold hand, as if he had something on his mind, but I pulled it back to keep him from saying anything, and we walked together toward the bow.

As we threaded our way into the shrubbery, I had the sudden sensation that the cold of thousands of years of accumulated snow on the peak of Bala's Dream was making its way into my body through billions of pores. The wind was beating against my body as though I were naked. Hunching my shoulders to keep the cold out, I wanted desperately to turn and go back, but I couldn't come up with an excuse. Yan Lun gave me a brief look of masculine gentleness that I hadn't imagined possible—a sign of pity, perhaps—and whispered, Want to go back?

I nearly threw myself into his arms to vent a bellyful of grievances, but since I was used to treating men I could never love with extraordinary indifference and resolve, I simply shook my head. He responded, with a mixture of confusion and impatience, by taking a coarse wool sweater out of his backpack and putting it around my shoulders. The ancient mountain path was becoming less well defined and more treacherous. The uneven stones placed here and there were murder on my feet, as if I were stepping on brambles. Both sides of the path were dotted with the sunbaked white skeletons of men and beasts, one of which, I was convinced, must have been mine. Maybe that proved I'd already lived my allotted span of years, that I'd experienced all conceivable emotions countless times, and that to continue on would be boringly redundant. But if that were the case, why practice my feminine wiles on a driver? Could it be that the act of walking into such a forsaken valley, my mood changing from one moment to the next, proved that the turmoils of my life hadn't ceased? Or that there was something I still coveted? The pain in my feet soon got so bad that I stopped and sat down on a dry pile of bones, refusing to go on.

You'll freeze to death if you stop.

Are you hungry?

Do you have to relieve yourself?

He circled round me, trying to guess why I'd stopped. I took some delight in seeing his anxiety, although I didn't show it, and just shook my head indifferently. He continued trying to get me up and moving, but when he realized that his words were falling on deaf ears, he turned angrily and started walking up the mountain alone. But I knew he'd come back, a sentimental young man with a fondness for women. So why was I trying to make a youngster still wet behind the ears suffer emotionally? Angry with myself, I jumped to my feet and caught up with him, where I smiled as though nothing had happened. That single action so moved him that he slipped my heavy backpack off and flipped it over his own shoulder. Then, to make amends, he ripped a branch off a tree and handed it to me.

Use this as a walking stick, he said. It'll make it easier going up the mountain. I'll walk ahead and keep the path clear of snakes.

The sky turned dark so quickly it took me by surprise, and night was nearly upon us. The light of fireflies filled the sky with falling stars, creating the illusion that I'd entered a heavenly palace. But when I lifted my eyes and gazed up at the dark silhouettes of mountain peaks ahead and heard the howling of wolves and the screeching of monkeys off in the distance, the comforting sensation of being in a heavenly palace vanished. A wolf's howl pierced the sky and sent shivers up my spine. Yan Lun apparently sensed it and said, as though he were calming a child, There aren't many wolves in the forest because bird droppings rot their skin. That's enough to keep them out. Wolves have lots of different calls, from guttural to shrill, sounding sometimes far and sometimes near. But don't worry, I've got a gun.

Wordlessly I followed him, one uneven step after the other. I had no idea where we'd be spending the night, but since I'd made up my mind to go with him into the mountains, I was mentally prepared for anything.

Hunters often spend the night in this cave. Yan Lun led me into the gaping, toothless mouth of a cave as though I were a calf or a kid. A strange, pungent odor assailed my nostrils and made me sneeze. He struck a match and lit a candle. After taking a look around, he said with authority, Someone was here not long ago. The smell of burnt moxa and orpiment grass is still in the air.

What for?

Poisonous snakes hate the smell.

My heart was in my mouth, but this calmed me down. I've always been terrified of snakes. I'd rather stand face to face with a tiger than run across a snake. He laid a sheet of oilcloth out on the ground for me, then took my clothes out of my backpack and told me to put them on—all of them. He sat at the mouth of the cave after lighting two campfires next to me, telling me to get some sleep so I could relieve him in the middle of the night.

Why don't we both sleep?

Wolves will come if the fires go out.

Let 'em come.

A sneer spread across his face, then his eyelids drooped as if he were going to sleep; he ignored my comment. I was so tired I expected to fall asleep as soon as my head touched the ground, but instead I lay there wide-awake for a long time.

An eerie silence filled the night, and my chilled body seemed to melt into the inky blackness until all that was left was a bloody heart struggling to get out of the deep abyss of the bed. Moans like those of a sick dog emerged from Father's bedroom, melting my heart and stopping its beating. A hundred days ago Father had been grief-stricken as he'd held Mother in his arms on her deathbed. After her cremation, he stood in a daze on the balcony from sunset to sunrise. Try to put Mother out of your mind, I said. We can't go on living just to suffer. He hugged me with a deep sense of gratitude. I knew you'd say that. You're a lot more enlightened than I, and more worldly. He was too relieved and happy to notice the pallor in my face and the trembling of my lips. As he left, I gazed at his back, all stooped from his learning and his position. I don't know how long I sat there in a sort of daze.

He came home—the husband who had worn out shoe leather and knocked himself out trying to find a way for us to settle in Scandinavia.

Have you finished your thesis? Why don't you turn on the light? He flipped on the light switch.

I shook my head, hoping against hope that he'd come over, take me in his arms, and ask why I was unhappy. But no, he was too excited. The Swedish woman has agreed to write a formal invitation letter. Help me get some clothes together, sweetheart. I'm taking her to Guilin tomorrow.

Guilin? Why didn't you say something earlier?

Because I know I have an enlightened, worldly wife. He put his arms around me, gave me a perfunctory kiss, and held my hand.

I'm tired. I pulled my hand away.

Then go to bed. I'll do my own packing.

I climbed into bed. He threw some things into a bag and left. When I saw the carefree look on his face as he was packing, I suddenly recalled the scene at the Swedish woman's apartment a few days earlier: I had knocked several times before she came to the door. Her aging face was as red as a lobster. Panic was written all over it. Her cheeks were flushed.

He, he's taking a bath . . . So forced, so unnatural.

Is my wife here?

He walked into the room, cool and collected, a bath towel wrapped around his waist. The sound of his booming voice and the sight of his glowing face unnerved me.

Sit down, please. His relaxed manner put her at ease.

As soon as I get dressed, dear, let's take Kathy home for some wontons. He turned and gave the old woman a broad grin. My wife's an expert at making wontons.

I wasn't sure if he was really relaxed or just putting on a show. But if I turned and walked out now or let my suspicions show, given the atmosphere he'd created, I'd have been thought of as awfully narrow-minded or extremely rude. So all I could do was look on benignly as he helped her downstairs by holding her arm, and then as he taught her how to use chopsticks by wrapping his hand around hers. Searching deeply into my own heart, I asked myself, Was I really and truly calm? What frightened me was the thought that to be otherwise would be blasphemous. He was waiting on the poor old Swedish woman so attentively it made her head spin. How well I knew that women like that, who were old enough to be my mother, could accommodate all the affection bestowed upon them by "ethnics" and more, which made them easy picking for Chinese men. This old woman, born and bred in Scandinavia, had a flirtatious look in her eyes from start to finish.

My husband fell asleep, abandoning me to the darkness of

our bed. He'd pecked me on the cheek as he turned out the light, completing his bedtime routine, sort of like flashing an ID card to the guard as he entered his office. He was so healthy, so spirited, so purposeful, so orderly; he had an easy grip on the reins of his life. Never swayed by his emotions, or the attitudes of others, or expressions of tenderness, or a woman's tears; to him these were no more significant than a bottle of soy sauce. Once his objective was fixed, he moved toward it with single-minded determination. The cost of this single-mindedness, of course, was the unavoidable loss of the essence of true emotion. His response to that? Everything has its price. Not a care in the world. His life was clear-cut and trouble free. And me? My slothful idleness wearied and bored me. I was such a nervous wreck I couldn't fall asleep nine out of ten nights. Sometimes I was so tired I lay there in a half sleep tormented by nightmares. And even on those nights when I did manage to fall asleep, I'd wake up feeling more tired than when I'd gone to bed. The sight of my husband sleeping so soundly beside me usually made me jealous and spiteful. How could he appreciate the torment of insomnia?

One night I was in such a state I told him that my insomnia terrified me, that it was like crawling down into a blood red snake pit in the middle of the night. He had a good laugh over that, wondering why he'd never known that his wife had a novelist's imagination. He was snoring again before the echo of his words died out. I shook him awake and snarled, Someday you'll know what it means to suffer! He was so stunned by my outburst that his sleepy eyes suddenly came to life. He sat up and smoked half a pack of cigarettes, one after the other, in complete silence. That was probably the first wakeful night he'd spent in all his thirty-five years. And yet he got up bright and early the next morning, rested and full of pep, looking like he'd completely forgotten the events of last night. My angry outburst had distressed me, but to him it was nothing. She's like a child who refuses to grow up, he joked to my father. She's even terrified about losing a little sleep. Was he trying to give me an easy way out, or did it just never quite register with him? To this day I still don't know.

17

The moans of a sick dog from Father's room had stopped, and were replaced by a blend of heavy breathing. They were asleep; so was my husband, and so was the rest of the city. They'd enjoyed another day in this tumultuous world, and were now in some other world where tranquillity reigned, leaving me to keep watch over the night in my weary state. I was all alone. I was angry. My heart was a lamp whose oil had been used up. Why was I waiting for yet another identical night, another identical day? Why didn't I take possession of that eternal serenity? Did I want to see that old face with the flushed cheeks again? Did I want to hear the nightly moans of a sick dog? Or did I want to cling to a love no one possessed, yet which everyone was trying to manufacture and sell? Surrounded by darkness, I put my fingers on my jugular vein . . . it was throbbing. In the bright sunlight it would be a seductive blue color. What was that, was my hand shaking? Maybe I needed to take another look at my husband. He was sleeping like a baby, dreams of traveling to Scandinavia swirling around his pillow. That brutishly healthy spirit had once roamed leisurely all over my glorious body; naturally it had also warmed itself at my feet for years, like a cat next to a stove. Our terrifying lovemaking had blossomed in body and spirit, and we had suffocated in the emotional needs of something we mistakenly called love. But that had soon been relegated to history, until all that was left were two aging machines moving at different speeds. With an aching heart, I took out the packet that lay in preparation, got dressed, and tiptoed into the study, where I lay down on the sofa. My hands were shaking uncontrollably, but inside I was extraordinarily calm . . . it was the decree of fate: only an extremely sensitive body could win him over. Maybe we were born to be a couple, the embodiment of yin and yang. The toilet flushed with a loud torrent of water, as though in response to something, and he appeared in the doorway of the study fastening his belt around his trousers. What's wrong? Can't sleep again?

As I looked with a blank expression at the crude smile on his face, so much grief welled up in my heart that I couldn't utter a word.

I walked out of the cave at dawn and discovered that we were on a strangely captivating mountain slope. Through the pink morning fog, I could see petrified sparkling coral, water plants, and sea cucumbers all around. Deep blue reefs spread out from the peak above me down the slopes like cascading waterfalls. A solidified ocean had been wrenched free and transported here to form a mountain. I was so moved and shaken by the sight that I could only stand there in muted, staring stupefaction. I sensed some movement behind me, and when I turned to look, Yan Lun was kneeling amid the campfire smoke and swirling morning fog. Silky blue ribbons of smoke drifted toward me, rising effortlessly into the air, getting whiter and whiter, finally merging with the reddish morning fog. With all my heart I believed that this lyrical dawn in the mountain forest and Yan Lun, enveloped in the lyrical smoke, had been sent by a holy spirit to caress this weary being and this heart that had roamed too far. I clasped my hands together and gave silent thanks.

Who are you praying to?

The earthly sounds of Yan Lun's voice shattered the holy serenity of the moment.

After breakfast it'll take us a couple more hours to reach the peak.

As though my soul had taken flight, I absentmindedly ate a few bites of food, then followed him into the woods. On and on we walked, and when we emerged from the woods, a path like a white thread stretched out ahead of us between two cliffs. Yan Lun said, This path was formed by the hooves of wild horses. Walking along the path gave me the sensation that something wondrous was about to occur. It kept getting narrower and narrower, until halfway up the mountain it could barely accommodate my steps. Precipitous cliffs rose up on both sides as the path twisted and turned in its ascent up the mountain, and every step was fraught with the danger of plunging into a seemingly bottomless abyss. At a spot where the path curved like the horn of an animal, I suddenly spotted a dozen or so wild horses heading straight for us. The path was too narrow to step aside, and there was no turning

19

back, so we just stopped in our tracks. The leader of the pack, a powerful stallion, also stopped, followed by the horses behind him. We stood our ground facing each other on the perilously narrow path. Yan Lun, clearly nervous, grasped my hand without a sound and took a quick look all around. Screaming or shedding blood in the surrounding green tranquillity—green mountain, green forest—would be blasphemous. I grew calm and cast a friendly look at the pack of horses. Unlike people, who seem so different from one another, they were all very much alike: white bellies, white jaws, and patches of white on their backs. Faint stripes on their bodies glistened in the sunlight. There was something unusual about them: no ordinary pack of wild horses, they were rare creatures of the forest. I said nothing as I stood there in fearless excitement. Yan Lun looked over at me, his face taut as he fought to control the panic in his heart. He coughed and said softly, Don't be afraid. I'm right here.

I was so deeply immersed in awe of the wild horses I barely heard what he said. Then, thank God, with extraordinary agility and goodwill, they turned around, one after the other, and retreated to a wider spot on the path, where they stopped and pressed themselves up against the cliff to give us room to pass, which we did. Once we'd squeezed past them, they followed us for a short distance out of curiosity before stopping and watching us make our way up the mountain. Maybe they were fulfilling a mission, or maybe it was their first encounter with two-legged creatures, but there was an unmistakable look of affection in their unsullied eyes. I don't know how to describe what was in my heart at that moment, or how to interpret this encounter. But my heart began to ache and my eyes reddened.

Don't be afraid. We're safely past them.

Yan Lun was comforting me to ease his own nervousness. He put the walking stick back into my hand and smiled slightly as a sign that his masculinity was still intact.

The peak's covered by snow, so I'll help you negotiate the climb when the going gets tough.

I followed him in silence.

Damn! I left my red scarf back in the cave.

Yan Lun's outcry threw a scare into me.

I took it out last night to look at it, and before I went to sleep, I hid it in the pile of moxa . . . he paused as his face reddened to the roots of his ears. Avoiding my eyes, he said, I have to go back and get it.

You can't! It's too far, and too dangerous.

But he'd already taken off running down the thin white thread before the sound of my voice had died out. Since I had no way of probing this mystery, I decided to lie down on the mountain slope to rest. In less than an hour he returned, his face covered with excitement and sweat. He ran up to me shouting breathlessly, I found it!

Let's see!

Uh-uh.

Oh, I understand.

I didn't mention the red scarf again as we continued up the mountain. But he was bursting to tell me, and finally did. He told me how he'd met a girl in Bala village, how she'd been his guide in the forest when he went to find the old professor, how she'd brought down a mountain goat with a single arrow, how she'd bathed him in a mountain stream, how she'd loved red scarves, how she'd shown him a night he'd never forget, how she'd secretly bought a red scarf in the town of Purple Lady . . . we scaled the peak of Bala's Dream in the company of his happy reveries.

How many millennia had this snow lain there? How deep was it? Impossible to know. All I could see before me was a shining, impenetrable crust of ice that completely enveloped the nearby peaks like a huge wave, turning them into an enormous multihued tower of ice. I felt as if I'd been placed atop a gigantic lens that reflected the colors of the sun's rays. Everywhere I looked I saw a profusion of rainbows—flashing, separating, merging, and vanishing. As far as I was concerned, this place was the epitome of brilliance, a temple of brilliance. The moist, heavy clouds were surprisingly low, so close it seemed I could reach out and rip off a piece. They were like silent waves billowing over our heads. When I looked around, I noticed that the sun was right in front of me on the horizon, above the dazzling glacier and below the

21

moist, heavy, deepening red. Unable to control my excitement any longer, I fell down in the snow, a bundle of naked overheated passions, to burn like an inferno on the peak of this glacier. I wanted to disgorge all the effluvium in my belly and fill it with the gentle fragrance of the mountain-forest greenery. I wanted to shout to the mountain range in its eternal solitude, Here I am——

But before I could get the words out, a feathered arrow whizzed past my eyes and stuck in the ice above and slightly to the left of my head. The tip was so incredibly sharp it made hardly a sound as it stuck and sent out hardly any chips of ice; a shaft of cold light pierced my heart. I scrambled to my feet and pulled the arrow out of the ice. I shivered.

Who's there? Yan Lun instinctively pulled back the bolt of his rifle.

Whoosh—— Another arrow stuck in the ground at his feet. We were terrified, not knowing where the arrows had come from. Just then a lean, wiry man leapt from his hiding place and landed threateningly right in front of us. He was barefoot and wore only a golden-striped leopard skin over his loins. A shiny black bow was slung over his shoulder. He stood there, seemingly unaffected by the ice beneath his bare feet.

It's you?

The dark rays of his eyes were like the spreading talons of a hawk, ready to pounce on me. He pointed to the sky, then made signs to the ground, shouting incomprehensibly; one of his fingers nearly stabbed me in the mouth.

What do you want! Struck by a sudden inspiration, Yan Lun fired a shot in the air.

Startled by the crack of the rifle, the man cast Yan Lun aside and shoved me to the ground, then curled up into a ball and rolled into a hollow in the ice. Just as Yan Lun was about to tear into him, he was stopped in his tracks by a tremendous rumbling all around. The dense clouds above us merged and roiled, then turned black all of sudden and began to settle upon us darkly. While the glare of incinerating bolts of lightning was still in the air, our scalps were rattled by earsplitting thunder. Wind and rain and thunder and lightning filled the sky and covered the earth. Raindrops the size of peanuts, wrapped in the protection of the wind, crashed painfully down on our heads and faces; my scalp turned numb and I saw stars. The curled-up fellow was looking at me through his crotch and grinning, and no matter how I ran around and screamed, he remained utterly impassive. Yan Lun was dashing around in a daze, frantically trying to find a place to hide, ultimately bumping into me, and sending us both crashing to the ground. Holding me tightly, he shielded me with his body. The rain ran down my collar and under my clothes, slicing my face like a razor. The earth seemed to be splitting apart, trying to escape from certain death. My head was buried in a watery tomb, and I was so panic-stricken I could barely breathe. My heart convulsed from fear, exhaustion, physical weakness, and asphyxiation. I passed out . . .

I regained consciousness at dusk under the blood red rays of the setting sun, and the first thing I saw was a deep purple column of stone. It glistened in the fading rays of the sun like a pillar of oily flesh, so seductive I had an irresistible urge to reach out and touch it.

It wasn't stone; it was a pillar of flesh! I drew back my hand fearfully, not daring to believe my surroundings—fresh flowers, hedge bamboo, mango trees, young maidens in sarongs. I couldn't help reaching out to touch it . . .

Hah, I thought it was a stone column, too. Are you awake?

Yan Lun was sitting on a bamboo fence beside me, wiping my face with a hot towel. He turned and shouted something toward a bamboo hut nestled in a grove of trees. I didn't understand the dialect, but I knew he was informing the owner of the hut that I'd come to. The lean, wiry man appeared in the doorway of the hut. He'd changed into a dark blue sarong and sleeveless jacket. His gaunt, dark face exuded a deep green radiance. He was like a torch burning with a green flame, burning its way straight toward me. I bowed my head instinctively, afraid that the hawk's talons would rip my heart to shreds. He walked toward me without making a sound, and the strong scent of the mountain threw me into a panic, nearly destroyed my composure. I looked up to see his coarsely sewn sarong fluttering in front of my eyes.

23

I shivered slightly, as a haughty indifference immediately enveloped my vibrant female body like a suit of armor. My heart was mocking me. I gazed at him with the ordinary look of someone watching animals grazing in a zoo or a nature preserve. He offered me a bamboo cup filled with wine, but I refused it with a shake of my head. In order to lighten the atmosphere, Yan Lun accepted the cup, from which he took a drink and smacked his lips in appreciation.

He says we shouldn't shout on the mountain, and that it's dangerous to fire a gun. There's some sort of, what is it . . . an enormous bay across the way, and the mist that rises from it gathers over the valley, where it forms clouds that are saturated with water . . . right, now I remember. That old professor told me the same thing. Drink a little wine, it'll warm you up.

I took the cup from him and, after wiping the edge with my handkerchief, took a tiny sip, then handed it back to the lean man. He took it from me, turned and headed back to the hut without a word. Almost immediately two girls came toward us, their bracelets and anklets clanking as they walked. One of them had a bamboo bowl in her hands. The moment he saw them, Yan Lun rushed over to one of them like an attack dog, grabbed her hand, and said excitedly in Mandarin, It's you! Quickly changing to another language, he muttered something and gestured animatedly with his hands. The girl shook her head vigorously, and I could see there was no recognition in her deep-set eyes, which had lit up at the sight of a man. She was so seductive, with quivering breasts and buttocks straining to burst through her tight-fitting sarong and sleeveless jacket. Her full, red lips parted slightly, then closed. I could see she had no idea who he was, a real blow to his ego. He muttered something else and gestured some more before reaching into his breast pocket and taking out the red scarf, the sight of which made her heart blossom like the spreading tail feathers of a peacock. She trembled from head to toe as she took the scarf from him, tied it around her slim waist, and swayed her hips provocatively, then used it to tie up her loose hair. She didn't take her eyes off Yan Lun for a moment, and it was clear that her actions stemmed from the

24

fact that Yan Lun was a man, or that she'd fallen in love with the red scarf, and not that there'd ever been anything between the two of them. But it was enough to restore Yan Lun's self-respect. There was a look of rapture in his eyes.

I was amazed by the unashamed femininity of these women, who could arouse a man without even trying. This was especially true of the one standing off to the side holding the bamboo bowl and looking as seductive as humanly possible, even though Yan Lun clearly didn't have his eye on her. Her breasts were heaving even more sensually than the other girl, and there was a flirtatious look in her eyes as her hips swayed provocatively. But poor Yan Lun was oblivious to it all. He turned and said distractedly, You'll stay with her. Her grandmother's from the interior and knows a little Mandarin.

With that he turned and walked arm in arm with the first girl into a grove of banana trees. The girl holding the bamboo bowl walked reluctantly up beside me and sat down on a dark purple log.

Here, eat. She managed a couple of words with difficulty.

It gave me a sense of extraordinary intimacy, which only increased the sense of isolation in this foreign place.

What race do you belong to?

She shook her head as I took the bowl from her. She was blushing as she looked away.

Does this hut belong to your family? Is he your husband? Hm? Your man? I pointed to the lean man, who was skinning a mountain goat by the steps.

She cocked her head, then shook it. But then she stole a glance at me, muttered Um, and nodded her head, and I took her ambiguous response as a sign that she didn't want to reveal any secrets. So I let the matter drop.

Why is this log we're sitting on so shiny?

I was just trying to make conversation, but she blushed from embarrassment. She rested her head bashfully on her chest and didn't say a word. Now more puzzled than ever, I wondered how she could be so open and natural in front of a man, but incurably bashful around a member of her own sex.

The sun was setting in the mountain valley to the west, throwing the charming village of Bala into darkness. The mountain peaks, the bamboo thickets, and the girl in front of me turned to black and white. I was suddenly afraid, experiencing for the first time the feeling of being far from home. Before this there'd always been a piece of familiar ground beneath my feet, and all I had had to do was step on it to feel my roots and be at peace. Ah, home.

The girl came over and helped me to my feet, then led me up the steps into the spacious hut, which was divided by strips of bamboo into two rooms. Except for a large stove, the outer room was completely empty, but the walls of the inner room were covered with bows and arrows, hunting rifles, animal pelts, and the dried skulls of all kinds of animals. A thick, woven rug lay on the floor amid a pile of bones and antlers, on which the lean man was stretched out. His eyes were half closed, and he didn't open them as we entered the room. The woman rummaged around the room for a moment, as if he weren't there, and pulled an identical rug out of the pile of stuff. She laid it out in the outer room, then pointed first to me, then to herself, meaning that she and I were to sleep on it. I nodded to show I understood. She fetched a bucket of water, then made a series of hand gestures. Wish? she said with difficulty, which I took to mean I was to wash up. But how was I supposed to get undressed and wash in front of the porous bamboo partition between me and the fellow lying in the inner room? Assuming I hadn't understood, she said Wish? again, with the same difficulty. But I shook my head and lay down fully dressed, and when she saw I wasn't going to wash up, she quickly got undressed and stood up against the bamboo partition stark naked, then picked up the bucket of water and poured it over her head; the water flowed down her body and the bamboo. Having finished her bath, she dried off and walked into the other room without getting dressed, picked up a little wooden box and carried it over to our rug, where she knelt down.

You . . . What should I ask her? Her actions were so strange.

Um . . . blah, blah blah, blah . . . I didn't understand a word, nor could I tell what she was trying to say. But she smiled radiantly as she opened the box and removed a little mirror, which she placed in front of her. Then she took out a dozen or so pieces of colored charcoal and began drawing little green flowers and grass on her supple breasts. After that she drew twisting vines and tendrils in red, yellow, blue, and black from her breasts down to her navel. Finally around her navel, she drew a blood red circle, which spread brilliantly all the way to her inner thighs, where the straight lines seemed to twist and curve, and all the colors seemed to change places. The effect of the whole seductive design was so tantalizing that anyone, male or female, couldn't help but be aroused. The girl kneeling in front of me was transformed into a seductive mountain genie, a sacrament of love, a totem to sex! The look of astonishment in my eyes seemed to excite her, and she pointed to the colored charcoal, indicating I was to draw. My heart was pounding; my body was astir with an indescribable fervor. Me draw? No, my bedroom of hypocrisy was filled with pallor and drabness, and when I made love, my mind was usually somewhere else. She obviously thought that was too bad, but she gathered up the pieces of colored charcoal and put them back into the box, which she took into the inner room. When she came back, she lay down quietly beside me. Moonlight filtering into the room through the cracks in the walls and the window fell on our faces and bodies like warm, fragrant lips, making me yearn for a kiss. A subtle sadness spread over my soul as I saw the peaceful look on her face and the restless movement of the design on her body. I felt bad for her, and for myself. It was so peaceful I tossed and turned. By then I was probably a little feverish, so I peeled off my outer clothes, soaked by the rain and dried by the heat of my body, put on my white silk nightgown, and took off my underclothes beneath it. Finally, with a bitter taste in my dry mouth, I drifted off to sleep.

What was going on? The hut was shaking! Heavy breathing, moans, and shrill cries blended together. My eyes snapped open. She wasn't there beside me. I suddenly understood what lay behind her peaceful expression and the sultry designs on her body. I buried my face against the bamboo partition and held my breath to keep out the quivering odor of the bamboo. Some frenzied panting, a chilling cry, fol-

27

lowed by a turbid, heavy sigh, like every pore had opened as far as it would go to spill out the last drop of liquid . . . my hairs were standing on end, my body was pressed rigidly up against the bamboo partition. After a moment I broke into a cold sweat, as though a specter were passing over my body; my silk nightgown was soaked. Stillness returned to the inner room, and after I'd managed to calm down, I got to my feet and started out of the hut. When I reached the doorway, something made me turn back for a last look. What I saw was immediately etched on my heart forever, a truly unforgettable sight. The girl was lying up against the bamboo partition like a bucket whose water has been spilled out onto the ground; she was perfectly motionless, to all appearances dead. Maybe a woman's body reaches that degree of peace only after the ultimate climax. The man, having pushed the woman away, lay stretched out flat on the rug, his belly, hips, and groin covered with dark blue tattooed designs. In the silvery moonlight they looked like a pair of mating snakes that had coiled and wriggled as one. His muscles seemed to be infused with the potency of heaven and earth, as though the spirit of sex had claimed him for all eternity.

My heart had already begun to take flight, as though it were riding on the clouds. I walked out of the hut. Mountain peaks, night fog, hedge bamboo, mango trees, a dark green thicket of flesh . . . just as I pulled myself together, I spotted a girl covered with blood red designs sitting on the dark purple log. She sprang to her feet when she heard me approaching and started to run away. But then she saw who it was and went back to the log, where she sat down again, looking terrified. My heart felt as if it were in a vise and my teeth were chattering. Suddenly everything was crystal clear, but I could hardly believe it. If it hadn't been for the dense shadows of the hedge bamboo, I don't know where I could have gone to keep my confusion hidden from the light of the moon. Even though my eyes were shut, I could see among the whirling, dark green shadows the red designs on the women's bodies.

I don't know how much time passed before I heard the door bang and the footsteps of the lean, wiry man as he came down the steps. Before I had time to react, I heard what sounded like two full bottles coming sharply together. He was consumed by a red ball of fire, as two entwined bodies rolled into a grove of banana trees. Although I couldn't see clearly, I could feel the flames of movement in front of me . . . the forest was going up in flames, red and yellow tongues of fire were licking at me. I was on fire, the marrow in my bones was crackling, blood red flames shot from my eyes. She was already burned to a crisp, but who was she? The girl with the red designs? Or me? The cinders of my heart had obliterated reason and energy, and I was incapable of judging, unable to figure it all out. My footsteps had never been so light. The heaviness that had filled my heart and pressed down on me had vanished without a trace. I had ceased to exist, and was now molten metal, spewing showers of sparks, drawn to the magnet of the purple log.

Then something strange happened. The moment I reached the log, he waved his magic wand and appeared in front of me. His face was twisted; his eyes emitted a gloomy green light. My knotted heart was thumping violently against the frail wall of my chest. I had to open my mouth to gulp in breaths of air. Before I could scream, he ripped off my nightgown, bent down, grabbed my legs, and lifted me up against his chest upside down. Then he thrust his head between my legs like a hungry wolf, sucking, searching . . . I felt sucked dry until all feeling in my toes had nearly died. But then I was suddenly filled to bursting with shame and anger, disgust and revulsion.

You, what do you think you're doing! Ah——

As the scream left my throat it seemed to shatter my whole body. Suddenly fearful, he stopped what he was doing and let me drop to the ground. When he saw the look of rage on my face, he grinned broadly, exposing two rows of radiant white teeth. After brushing the dirt off his body, he turned and headed toward the hut as though nothing had happened. I lay there in the dense shadows of the hedge bamboo, badly shaken.

The sun shone brightly on the hut through the branches, on the mountains so green they seemed to ooze liquid, on the fresh flowers, on colorful butterflies, and on me as I lay crumpled alongside the purple log.

He was barefoot and bare chested, like before, a golden-striped leopard pelt girding his loins. A shiny black bow hung from his shoulder as he walked up the icy path into the woods.

The girls had washed the designs off their bodies and were dressed in their sarongs. They looked like peonies, bathed in the morning dew, blossoming vibrantly in the mountain wilds.

Yan Lun walked toward the hut, his face a study in exhaustion. When he saw me, he was so shocked he didn't know what to say. You?

I crossed my arms in front of me to cover my torn nightgown. Was I hurt? Ashamed? Angry? Sorrowful? No. I can't describe the feelings that bore down heavily on me and crushed me into powder. I threw myself into Yan Lun's arms, where I soaked his shoulder with my silent tears.

Who was it? Who did this to you? Beside himself, he wrenched free of my grip to run toward the hut.

But I held him back and shook my head. I was so choked by the bitter juices of suffering I couldn't breathe. The sounds of my sobs thundered across the valley and the forest.

I was so spent I was barely awake, so Yan Lun picked me up and carried me in his arms back down the path, away from Bala's Dream.

GREEN EARTH MOTHER

Earth Mother is the central icon in the Potala Palace, a mythical, benevolent Buddhist saint. She is said to have seven eyes, with which She can see into people's hearts. Her right leg is stretched out in symbolic suppression of anger and realization of mercy. Earth Mothers come in five colors—white, red, blue, yellow, and green—of which green is the most basic. A powerful roc with golden wings is perched atop the green Earth Mother's head; it is Her protector.

NIGHT ONCE AGAIN DECEIVED PEOPLE'S EYES. The wind relentlessly toyed with the overripe berries. In the orange morning light, Mimi pushed open the double cedar doors. The earth was blotted with the reddish-brown juice of crushed berries—already rotten, they hid a hope brighter than the eyes of birds in their hearts: now that winter had passed, who could stop the multicolored seeds from sprouting green buds? Mimi asked him about the ancient division of the seasons. Spring is spring winter is winter flowers bloom in the summertime fruit ripens on autumn days once you enter that time mountains rivers flowers trees wind clouds thunder lightning snow rain frost fog all things fuse or multiply even the excretions of men and women and boys and girls increase or decrease. He said it all in one breath.

Why?

People are powerless against the mysteries of Heaven and Earth. He put on a pair of greasy blue shorts and walked toward the inner room, his skin a snowy white. Mimi's heart floated softly along on two hairless, spindly legs. For days Mimi had been longing for a snowfall that would cover the land, freezing Heaven and Earth, solidifying the people in their places to keep their corrupt souls from fluttering all over the streets, even if her own heart was also frozen into a lump of ice. Mimi wanted to stick out her scalding tongue—I'll kiss you, kiss every pore on your body, suck in all the hidden flavors. Her tongue was already frozen. Ice and snow fused Heaven and Earth, embracing withered branches and dead leaves, wastelands and abandoned slopes, the bare stems of shriveled petals and the ancient forest far from the bustling city, its ruined, rust-blotched trees, and those aged, green-skinned people hobbling all over the world. The aged people wore an overcoat of snow as they seduced the young by singing the praises of parental love. Spring came, the snow slunk away to reveal the ravaged land in all its ugliness. Beneath the sun's rays, it shed tears as it related a tale of short-lived purity and a false love it should never have known.

Kiss me. Why are you afraid of Her?

It just isn't right.

It's not fair. Just look at Her wrinkled old mouth that has been stamped by hundreds, thousands of full-blooded lips, a once rosy color that has peeled away completely from countless scrapings. A kiss, you have to kiss me in front of Her.

It's as out of place as wearing a bathing suit on the street. The sound of his voice shriveled into a lump; the words ran together.

It's as ridiculous as wearing a mandarin gown in a swimming pool.

Blasphemous, sacred motherly love!

I want what's mine, it's got nothing to do with Her!

Okay, tonight we'll go to some deserted spot . . .

No, I don't want any more stolen kisses in the dark.

Mimi got up out of the bathtub, every pore on her bright pink body spreading open willfully, steam obscuring the reflection of her tender fresh naked female body in the dressing mirror. She pressed her face against the cold silvery surface. Not a single wrinkle anywhere, especially on her pink forehead. In twenty-five years, nine thousand days and nights, those delicate lips had never tasted a bright shining kiss! What appeared to be an invisible dark hand in the mirror was thrust into Mimi's small narrow chest, where it stroked a weakly beating heart that was covered by a thick, heavy layer of dust. Two streams of hot tears gouged out two pale scars. In the darkness Mimi was hopelessly entwined by pity.

If She opened her eyes, a lover's kiss would immediately become a sinful intrigue.

If, in a world of respect for one's elders, there's no room for a kiss in broad daylight, I'd rather have languished in my mother's womb and never have opened my eyes.

Not so loud. Mother will hear. He was breathing hard, his every word chiseled on Mimi's heart.

Mimi composed herself and gazed at the pale tiny tightly closed mouth in the dressing mirror. Her pink body was cooling off, turning as pale as wax. A delicate hand glided down it from top to bottom as she mused, Maybe this doesn't belong to me. No . . . but maybe . . . Love knotted in her heart, spun a thread that circled the earth three times, maybe more. Mimi was sure that sooner or later the world would be destroyed—by love.

Are you crying? Are you . . . The words stuck in his throat and simply wouldn't come out. He put a towel printed with cats' eyes—red, yellow, blue, white—over Mimi's shoulders. She shook her head, raining tears onto the back of his hand. When Mimi was little, Mama had said she was born under a crying star, that she had come into this world with tears in her eyes. Grannie believed she was an unlucky child, so on snowy days she secretly fed her snowballs. Mimi's mouth was frozen open like a trumpet as she sang and sang and sang, never stopping. All Mama could do was buy a set of imported earplugs.

Are you crying again? His hand was lily white and supple, so soft it seemed boneless. He wiped away the tears on her cheeks, then carried her back to the bathtub and the hot water. He rubbed her back, massaged her shoulders, then let his supple hands rest on her trembling breasts. Beads of water dripped through his fingers. Ribbons of orange light filtered in through a dark green bamboo grove. The ribbons, like spirit threads, tied up her tender little heart as they swayed back and forth. Pricked by sharp leaves, her heart settled like a fine powder over her childhood dream world, with all its colored lamps. The colored lamps congealed into a swarm of moths. The moths greedily sucked up the orange-colored light, which shone through their transparent wings. Mimi had been afraid of the moon's orange rays ever since she was little.

Knock-knock. She was at the door.

I'm taking a bath. What do you want?

Is he in there?

He . . . Before she could get it out, he covered Mimi's lips with his boneless hand.

Say I'm not here. His mouth was boring into Mimi's ear.

Why?

I shouldn't be here while you're taking a bath.

I'm your wife, I share your bed. What's wrong with a bath?

Blasphemous . . . blasphemous, sacred motherly love.

Ptui! Pettiness is the true blasphemous love! Mimi kicked the tub over. A pair of purple slippers floated toward the door on the spilled water.

Ai! A heavy sigh from the other side of the door splintered Mimi's heart. She hadn't left. Instead She cupped a brilliant excuse in her hands. I bought you a *Moonlight Sonata* tape. Come out here and we'll listen to it together.

Ma——he was embarrassed beyond belief. A snow white back slipped through the cedar doors.

It's my chest, the same old problem. The moans of a sick cat outside the door.

Ma——I'll massage it for you.

Mimi stood barefoot next to the window. She tumbled into a sea of mist, floated off toward a deep canyon—compressed into a breathless speck of dust, her bloodless lips parted, she gazed up at the creases squirming in the sky. A ruined face like a piece of rotting wood appeared in the tattered vault of heaven. Mimi rubbed her wildly beating heart. What is it I still want? she asked herself. Why hasn't my heart ossified? In spite of herself Mimi looked down into the courtyard. That knifelike face spread out across a hairless, snow white chest. Mimi was thinking, The flowers in Her eyes are blooming at an angle, the clouds are drifting at an angle, people are walking at an angle. Her happiness spilled out of Her crisscrossing creases. Like the new bloom of a withered flower, Her face came back to life. Four spindly legs intertwined; two bodies folded together. As though she were watching a centipede, Mimi hid, trembling, behind the curtain. Soap bubbles kept popping; water spread silently in all directions . . . a pair of tiny feet, made plump by soap bubbles, stepped on the scarlet gravel. A shout—Mama—the orbs of her buttocks arched as she walked, arched and quivered as though restless animals were hiding in them. Arms thrust out in front of her, Mimi ran toward the churning white foam stretching out before her, leaving behind a trail of happy birds' nests with her feet. A pile of bubbles was created in a second; a drab blueness required countless millennia. She ran into it, a fleshy red butterfly toying with a boundless expanse of waves. As she swam ahead, the fleshy red became white, the blue became a deep green.

Oh Mama, the ocean isn't blue! Mimi raised her pudgy arms, threw them around Mama's youthful long neck and floated lightly upward, the weight of twelve years seemingly as light as a feather. Mama scooped little Mimi out of the water, cupping her like a living heart. Watery eyes spread open, a rose. You're twelve years old today. Taking you swimming in the ocean is Mama's present to you, because you never enjoyed the love of a father . . .

Mama! Two wet faces pressed together; a childish heart grew suddenly solemn. A ferocious wave crashed over them. Mimi swallowed a mouthful of seawater, brackish and salty. Mama staggered back to the beach cradling Mimi in her arms. She looked at the stunned expression on Mama's face and felt resentment, sadness. She never swam in the ocean again.

The first time Mimi saw him was on her second trip to the seashore. She was sitting alone on the beach staring up at the moon, a sheet of red paper stuck onto the canopy of heaven above the sea. She was laden with sorrow. He walked up and sat down beside her. The beach was deserted, the sand unbearably cold and cheerless. He spoke to Mimi in a disbelieving voice. You look just like Her, the same sadness, the same purity. She loves the moon, the early morning sun, Beethoven, Spinoza . . .

A poet?

No, unemployed. Gets by by doing odd jobs. She published a story when She was eighteen; at twenty She had a solo vocal recital, as a coloratura. But like ordinary women, She gleaned scraps of coal and carried manure buckets, all for the sake of Her son . . . his voice quickly faded out. Mimi's heart leapt into her mouth. The sea was unbelievably calm; all she could hear were the softly lapping waves and the violent beating of her heart.

Do you love Her?

I adore Her. My only goal in life is to make Her happy.

Mimi's heart crawled; her narrow chest began to swell. The broad expanse of the beach was nearly unbearable. She headed over to a shaded path that led to the shore. The thick branches of the towering kola nut trees were intertwined, their thick shade forming a dark umbrella over Mimi's head. He followed quietly behind her, as still as a shadow.

Who is She?

My mother.

Thunder roared; the moon was gone. In the pitch darkness he grabbed Mimi's hand and drew up next to her, purring like a cat. Her suspended heart settled back down, dissolving into millions of pearls of tribute. The "motherhood" memorial arch screened out the last traces of jealousy. All the emotions in the world could be written with only the words affection or filiality; otherwise it would be blasphemy. A bolt of lightning flashed between them; two twisted faces drew together. In the space of a minute, countless driven raindrops crashed into two bodies and two hearts consumed by flames at the base of an ancient tree. They saw nothing, they heard nothing. There was only the driven rain and the mud and an inextinguishable fireball. Tens of thousands of years ago, the heavens had opened up angrily, just like tonight, and a pair of lovers had died for love beneath the branches of this ancient tree. After tens of thousands of springs, tens of thousands of summers, two carnal-colored seeds had formed deep beneath the roots of this gnarled, ancient tree. Maybe the vows would be answered on this rainy night, and the two love seeds would finally germinate and sprout forth. As the rain fell, they exchanged their burning hearts, which sizzled with each raindrop. A chill wind brushed past, whipping up flames of joy. Thunder roared angrily; the gigantic canopy of the tree rose into the air, then crashed to the ground. Their souls flew out of their bodies. The fire was out, but gray smoke continued to curl upward. The wind died down, the rain stopped, a cluster of rice-colored stars was set free to cleanse the canopy of heaven. They stared silently at one another like a pair of clay statues, gazing into each other's expression, all genuine feelings now lost.

Come to my place and change into some dry clothes.

No, Mother's waiting anxiously for me to come home.

They held hands tightly in the darkness, then let go. No words of comfort, no good-byes as they parted.

He knew it had been an extraordinary rainy night, and that he'd given her an even more extraordinary love. Mimi knew it had been a soul-stirring rainy night, and that she'd relinquished soul-stirring emotions to the rainy night. The rainy night had incurred a heavy debt. What they'd taken from the rainy night could never be easily abandoned. Love had turned their hearts into a scorched mass, but they remained fused together to avoid the pain of being ripped apart.

Mother wants to meet you.

Why?

She has to give Her permission for me to marry. I know She'll like you.

On Sunday he climbed the Great Wall, Mimi holding his left hand, Mother holding his right. He used up a roll of color film beside the North Sea, his left arm around Mimi's shoulder, his right hand gripping Mother's arm. Mimi let him hold the parasol, She handed him her feather-light handbag; Mimi took off her jacket and put it over his shoulders, She put her half-eaten popsicle up to his mouth; Mimi could see resentment in Her eyes, She could see superfluousness in Mimi's face. He tried to please Mimi by buying a popsicle, he tried to please Her by buying a soft drink, all the time panting like a cat in heat.

At dusk Mimi's first glance took in Her thick black hair, oppressive, impenetrable. Three pink moles at the corner of Her mouth were so close together they were almost one. From then on unlucky omens began to appear in Mimi's dreams. Bright red, meaty growths appeared. Countless pink eyes hidden in Her thick black hair, shedding tears like blood . . . Mimi often woke from her dreams in terror; in the surrounding blackness, she refreshed her image of him by looking through photographs.

How about this one?

No, you can't see Ma's disposition in it. This one's no good, either. You can't see Mother's grace in it. Um-um, these are even worse . . .

This one's pretty good.

Her hair isn't dyed.

Gray hair's a sign of kindness.

No, She looks too old. Mimi, under no circumstances are you to let Mother see this photo!

Why?

If She sees Herself looking so old, She'll be upset. From now on you're not to call Her an old lady to Her face. His words were strings of water drops that seeped into Mimi's heart like poison. Mimi's nerves felt raw; she was trembling. She walked out of the house and wandered aimlessly. She walked up to a shop where people were selling all kinds of diapers; countless wrinkled chapped feet stepped over pudgy babies lying on the ground as they fought over the colorful diapers. Mimi reached out. Four huge cats' eyes bit down painfully. She pulled her hand back and realized that her face was still pressed up against the icy window. She stared at the orange moon as it scurried in and out of a jumbled mass of clouds. Another daydream! Mimi dragged her stiffened legs out the door. What was this, a blanket of stars in the sky above and on the ground below? Heaven and Earth, everything was all jumbled up! Her face was soaked; water filled her eyes. She stepped in a puddle, shattering it as an orange moon landed on her instep. She kicked it away and walked up to the room, stepping in one puddle after another. Mimi stood in the doorway, oblivious to the passage of time. His broad, heavy back blocked her view of the reclining chair. They couldn't see Mimi, but Mimi could see his limp, boneless hand massaging a mound of withered, yellowed wrinkles. Amid the wrinkles countless stringy mammary glands converged to form two dark purple nipples, like overripe squishy grapes.

The pain in my chest started when I was pregnant with you. Her voice seemed to float up from the depths of a dying well, then sank slowly back down. Mimi could see Her parted lips, Her half-closed eyes, the three pink moles quivering in a red tide.

Ma, it feels better when I massage you, doesn't it?

Much better. Your head was so big it was a very hard delivery. For two days and three nights, that wretched father of yours never showed his face at the delivery room door. I was so angry I couldn't eat. My stomach ached from hunger . . .

Ma. Grief and indignation caused the big pale boneless hands to dig in too hard. The overripe purple grapes oozed two drops of pus-colored liquid. They hung there on the verge of falling off, quivering drops of muddy yellow, like a secret mixture of splendor and decay fighting off death. Mimi suddenly saw in the glass her own ghostly image.

Ai, you're all grown up. But I still remember what you were like as a child. You nursed at my breast every night and listened to me read *Snow White*. You didn't blink. Remember? I spanked you once because you stole Leilei's hanky, and you curled up in my lap and cried half the night. Pretty soon I started crying, too. Ai . . . words gradually gave way to soft moans.

Ma——the two mounds of withered yellow wrinkled skin were getting hot from the rubbing, turning red. His hands hesitated; they began to tremble. Terrified, he stared at the overripe, oozing purple grapes . . .

Mimi threw the towel over her shoulders, burst into the room, and stood there ramrod straight, beads of water streaming down her body.

You! The big pale boneless hands froze above Her chest.

All rubbing motions stopped for a full two minutes.

Reluctantly She opened her eyes. After a momentary fright She calmed Herself down.

What's wrong with you? He quickly picked up the sheet to cover up Mimi's naked body. As though awakened from a dream, Mimi cast a flustered look at her own dripping body, knocked his hand away, and recoiled to the side.

I told you long ago she's got emotional problems. Look at her, the poor thing. You stay here; I'll take her to the hospital. A look of great compassion on Her face.

No. Mimi huddled next to him and gripped his hand tightly.

Mimi, go to the hospital with Mother and let them see what's wrong, okay?

Mimi looked at him as though he were a stranger for a moment before jerking her hand free and throwing off the sheet that covered her. She ran to her own room, stepping on the rays of starlight. The bed was swirling, she buried her head in the fluffy pillow, her eyes were tightly shut. He held Mimi in his arms. He could feel her trembling, but couldn't hear the sobs stuck in her throat. His body was wracked by a cold shudder that stabbed into his heart. Her long damp hair gave off steam that encircled the two faces. A sharp pain in his heart as he dug his fingernails into Mimi's flesh. Mimi shrunk into his embrace; for a long, long time her terrified eyes were glued to those fleshy big pale boneless hands. He peeled the wet strands of hair off her cheeks, touched her full lips. His muscles tensed as he nervously reached for her hand. Two limpid drops of water oozed out from under her tightly shut eyelids. Don't open your eyes, hold my hand. Let's find our way out of this dark green grove together. Pointed leaves cradled strings of last night's dewdrops, emitting light yellow rays. Don't reach out. Every dewdrop knocked to the ground is one more shattered heart. Pressed tightly together, they walked forward, hand in hand. Stillness reigned, broken only by the even sounds of their labored breathing. As he raised his head, his face was imprinted with golden splotches of light filtering through cracks in the dark green canopy above. So was Mimi's snowy white blouse.

Creeping forward cautiously, their shoulders bent, they made their way through the dark green grove, a pair of intertwining silk ribbons gliding back and forth like an empty emotion being poured into an empty heart.

Kiss me. In the translucent light of the sun, a pair of feet like those of a tiny animal rose up on their tiptoes. The pointed leaves rustled interminably, sending light yellow dewdrops cascading to the ground, shattered. His back blocked out the sunlight; a wall of darkness suddenly spread out before Mimi's eyes, probably because the lamp at the head of the bed was smashed. In a flash two naked bodies formed a scarlet forest. Mimi's mouth opened wide, fingernails dug into his back. No, don't, stop . . . don't stop. Mimi wanted to push him away, but she dug her fingers deeply into flesh that could have been his or could have been hers. Two vibrant lives formed a bright rainbow. Four eyes were tightly shut, blood-filled lips fused together, Heaven and Earth were about to explode, the ark was capsizing . . . Don't move! I hear something. Footsteps on broken glass, hobbling back and forth beyond the door. A swarm of ants gently raised up a berry; several little stars silently leapt onto the wet window ledge. Rain dripping from the eaves turned into fine drops, falling freely to the ground in threads. The berries were completely smashed, oozing crimson earth. Already rotten, they hid a hope brighter than the eyes of birds in their hearts; now that winter had passed, who could stop the multicolored seeds from sprouting green buds? The scarlet forest began to fade, gradually becoming a gloomy violet. Mimi's verdant heart suddenly withered and cracked; springtime fled without a trace.

Is she better? Her voice was soft and supple, like a rope twisted out of rubber.

Much better, Ma——He was desperate to convince Her that nothing had happened a moment ago.

Is she asleep?

She fell asleep long ago, Ma. Still desperate to convince Her, he turned on the light and opened the door. An icy hand descended on Mimi's forehead. Oh! She's feverish. Mimi raised her eyelids, which were nearly stuck together.

She saw a knifelike old face leaning over her, a glinting cold
light like the dead grasses covering a winter pasture in whose
roots were hidden the hope of rebirth for snakes and scorpi-
ons, ants and bugs. Mimi was like a spring that had been
stretched too far, its tension completely lost. The channels in
her heart slowed down, twisted; last night, so transparent,
would decompose where it stuck. She tossed down a green
stone. The echo from the bottom of her heart reverberated,
was still reverberating. I'm not sick! I'm not. Mimi sensed
that she was an emotional, kind-hearted sparrow silently
keeping watch over a nonexistent snake track in the darkness
of a vast forest. Deep autumn, when the birds fly south, and
Mimi no longer had the strength to cross the single-file
bridge of his heart. Profound sorrow wrapped itself around
her. All Mimi could do was cry.

Mimi, you're sick.

There are yardsticks all over the world, but not a speck of
land for me anywhere. Take my measure with Your yardstick,
take Your measure with mine.

What nonsense is that? Mimi. You really are sick.

She has no husband, I have no father. None of us has a
father.

Mimi, snap out of it. I love you, Mother loves you, too . . .
She loves . . .

She loves acting high and mighty the foreign superstition
of not going outside on Friday the thirteenth eating sausage
sandwiches even if they taste funny drinking coffee without
sugar destroying nerves that are already too fragile . . .

Why do you insist on making this relationship impossible!

The relationship is cruel enough already. At first I was
confident in my youth and my good looks, confident that no
one could replace the love of a wife. Heh-heh, I was wrong.
You'll never have the courage to cut the umbilical cord, and,
of course, that's what She's counting on. It's not enough just
to be your wife . . .

God damn that Freud and his theories!

No, it's more than that. It's castration. Most Chinese men
are swallowed up by maternal love. There's nothing left. I
want nothing. I'm leaving.

What nonsense is that? You're sick. Where do you think you're going?

. . . Mimi walked into the gray, misty dusk empty-handed.

You can't leave. He reached out, but grabbed only the empty dusk air, like an infant who's lost the nipple and stares into a great void.

Let her go and walk it off. She's just tired. She walked over abruptly and stood in his way, Her face suffused with the innocence of an eighteen-year-old girl.

Ma——she's still got a fever. She's talking nonsense. Now that he'd found an excuse, he was as excited as a drowning man reaching out to grasp a straw, someone who'd found the hope to go on living.

Take it easy. Nothing will happen. Her voice was thinner than paper.

Ma——he felt like crying, but he didn't, though his eyes were burning.

An ancient ugly dying forest way off in the corner of the dark green sky. Decrepit forked branches, so rusted they looked as if they'd never borne flowers or brought forth tender new buds—ancient trees forced to bear the stigma that they hadn't seen the color of green in thousands of years. Flocks of birds perching densely on the shaky forked branches were exchanging curses that birds have known since antiquity. Pair after pair of bulging eyes looked down on Mimi's life and her lives to come. Mimi was frightened out of her wits. She wouldn't choose this decaying den of spies as the place to end her life. She emerged from the forest and lay down on a desolate slope covered with years of loneliness. The grass around her was restless; the desolate slope lifted her up until she was floating in the air. Snakes and scorpions, bugs and ants lazily raised their heads, eyes heavy with sleep. Mimi was so tired she couldn't keep her eyes open. An icy softness kept brushing past her hands. There was a tautness in her belly, a weightiness, painful cramps. She undid her underwear and held her bulging belly with both hands, letting the first flakes of snow moisten the tiny new life. A momentary throbbing reminded her that the child would be born under the sign of the serpent. Why is there so much movement during a period of hibernation? A smile spread across Mimi's face, as tranquillity settled upon her once again.

It's snowing hard now, and Mimi still isn't home. I'll find her and bring her back to talk some sense into her. His reproach was filled with anxiety.

I won't allow you to talk sense into her. Let her calm down first. Who knows, maybe she went to her mother's home. Mother held his arm. Her withered, yellowing body blocked the huge cedar doors.

Ma, let me bring her back and give her a good talking to. He tried to wrench his arm free from Her grip, but She held on for dear life.

I won't allow you to frighten her! She shouted anxiously.

Ma——he pushed Her hand away and burst through the door.

Stop right there! She ran out after him, stumbled, nearly fell. He had no choice but to rush back and steady Her. Her mouth was open wide; She was gasping. She couldn't speak.

Ma——

I won't allow you to be rough with Mimi. It's cold out there. I'll go with you to find her. Suddenly calm again, She looked at him tenderly. He lowered his head to avoid Her eyes. His voice was so low he seemed to be talking to himself. She's still got a fever.

Mimi raised her leg—it was stiff from the cold. She didn't have the heart to stamp a footprint onto the translucent surface, though maybe that was the way for her to experience the pleasure of destroying purity. White sky. White snow. White night. Tender snowflakes translucent in the boundless translucence. Not a breath of wind. The flakes seemed to be floating in their prescribed spots, a scene of chaos, nihilism. This was Mimi's cherished hope—Heaven and Earth a single color. As she stood in the snow, she could no longer see herself. Fossilized bones glistened so brightly they dazzled her eyes; her terrified, trembling heart had petrified, been transformed into a heart-shaped green agate tossed onto the boundless snow all by itself. Don't open the door, people, give the world a chance to hold on to this pale, powerless purity! Hide under the snowbound roof to cry alone over your own death. Look, the sky is responding to human misery by sending down its symbol of filial piety—snow that covers the ground. In the snow-covered wilderness, only the emerald green agate awaits rebirth—maybe the tragedy of these two legs will be replayed somewhere else in the universe. Mimi was overcome by sorrow, but she was at peace. Inadvertently, she discovered a long piece of light purple silk rolling back and forth across the earth's crust with a soft tearing sound, leaving behind an eternal silence. Mimi had no sense of her own being, not even as a tiny snowflake. As she slumped slowly to the snow-covered ground, she saw the bright, snowy red of the ancient grove with its rusted trees. Flowers in full bloom were like huge tongues stretching up into the vault of heaven, sucking dry all the blood vessels, turning the anemic Heaven and Earth paler than ever. The delicate and beautiful ancient forest trembled in the dazzling snow, sending skyward a cloud of red mist . . .

He picked Mimi up, his face as dark as the earth. He gazed in stupefaction at Mother's silvery new teeth. A confused look on his face, the twin expressions of laughter and crying.

THE FINAL MYTH

A FOREST WITH NO TREES, THE AIR STIFLINGLY thick; the absence of everything had become unbearably heavy, she couldn't see the fingers on her outstretched hand, eyes were by now useless, her heart opened up memories she'd never had . . . she was like a huge upended snail floating in the liquid rays of the sun. A blast of heat; her pores spread open, little scarlet mouths consuming her. When had she begun floating in this pool of blinding liquid? When had she sunk into it? She didn't know; there was no time to know anything.

We've tried hemostats. They don't work.

Soft, muffled, boundless sounds drifted up from the earth floating somewhere, fairly gliding past her. Doctors and nurses drifted back and forth like patches of white mist. She knew they were there but couldn't see them. Who was holding her hand? A damp heat flowed from her fingers straight to her heart. She wanted to push it away, but forgot where her hand was. All she could remember were the kapok flowers covering the trees, so red they made her tremble. Just a brief look, but the scene indelibly etched on her heart.

Hey, pregnant woman, what's your name? Where do you work? Why won't you say anything?

All the lies had been told. Who wanted to tell the remaining truth who wanted to hear it? She didn't like asking questions, and hated being asked them herself. Her heart had long been anchored in that limpid dawn. When a person's life reaches this point, maybe all that's left is an organ in which the last shreds of sincerity reside. This thought flashed through her mind as she tried to shift her sore, weak buttocks.

47

The dark green drapes were pulled back gently by a large, hairy hand; the sun's rays struck his naked body like an explosion. A deep breath and the golden hairs on his chest shimmered like the radiance of a rooster crowing at dawn.

I love you . . .

Me too.

Two bodies like fleshy figurines intertwined passionately on the plush, blood red carpet one more time. His lips were searching in a damp hot passage; her crumpled coiled body spread abruptly open like a budding flower. Two sparkling black eyes were imprinted deep in the blue gaze. His kiss touched the depths of her heart, like a tiny, insignificant death. He smiled, sending fallen leaves flying in the air, leaving behind only a garden filled with twinkling flower buds. The parched fields of her heart were immediately transformed into a verdant expanse where shepherd boys played freely and gaily.

The patient's getting restless. Is her blood pressure falling?

Give her blood, give her oxygen.

The sound was like gossamer, like floating cotton, coating the vine-covered fields of her heart and fluttering in the breeze. She wanted to sneeze, she wanted to call out, but she couldn't move.

Take it easy, take it easy!

She's still conscious. Don't move.

A white mist enshrouded her face, then another. Her body began floating gently upward. The outline of a man descended above her, still and silent, standing in the shape of an arch.

Doesn't it tire you to stand like that?

Not as tall as standing straight, not as short as kneeling; life's perfect position.

Straighten up, live life to the fullest!

I love you because you've shown me life's greatest truth!

His voice was fleshy, dripping fat; his arched frame, seemingly wrung dry, now lay crumpled in a heap against the wall. Suddenly two eyes like tiny fireballs burned wantonly into her face; the arched frame entwined itself tightly around her, her light yellow skirt and blouse floated to the ground like falling petals, two bodies tumbling in a heat wave were pinned against a golden red, grassy knoll. Her eyes were lightly shut as she waited dreamily for that moment. He shouted in alarm:

Hey, you're not a virgin!

She opened her eyes, her nose twitched. Her gaze froze in the cold air and would not return. The colors of the grassy knoll, green in the spring, yellow in the fall, sparkled on her pale cheeks.

Aren't you, really? He sat up dumbstruck, his soul taking flight.

She removed the ring with the fish-eye gem from her finger and flung it into his sweaty slipper, then left the way she'd come, her face ghostly pale. That very evening, under that same dwarf Chinese toon tree, Mother divulged the secret of how she'd tricked Father.

Tell them her condition's critical.

She's got no family.

Write it on her chart. That'll keep us out of trouble.

Tongue depressor.

Smoke and fire: a profusion of tiny scalding hands tightened around her heart and lungs, her internal organs were scorched, death stretched out in front of her, rock solid. A disgusting smell of rubber was thrust up her nostril, like a trickling stream slowly engulfing a scorched body. There seemed to be breath in her body, and tears; she didn't have to know what was going on around her, she could see him standing alone in the dim light of the living room.

I've been waiting for you outside for a long time. I didn't dare come in until everyone else was gone. There's a new crop of cucumbers at the market, and I know they're your favorite.

These few terse sentences sent her back to her glorious eighteenth birthday—even the homeliest girl knows how glorious it is to be eighteen. At the window and through the cracks of the dilapidated peasant hut, dozens of imbecilic eyes stare with wonder at a little cake with eighteen candles; they wonder if it's a wedding ceremony or a funeral. The flickering candlelight dances on the smooth skin of her solemn face and casts a huge swaying shadow on the wall. Under the gaze of all those eyes, stored up the year round in this remote impoverished village, she is as proud as an empress or a princess. The cost of this pride, of course, is the loss of a chance to work in the city.

But why?

You corrupted the poor and lower-middle peasants with your bourgeois life-style! He repeated what the commune party secretary had said with a gnashing of his teeth.

She buried her face in his chest like a little girl and released a barrage of pampered mutterings and tears.

More dreams of being eighteen?

He stroked her heaving back with one hand and ran the other through her thick hair. The loose, long hair flowed freely through his fingers like a waterfall; she felt as if she were running into the wind or submerged in a clear brook, her long hair floating on the surface like spreading clouds. He touched the tip of her nose; it quickly turned the color of a rose, he touched her lips, they parted weakly. Ten magical fingers, normally so rough and rigid, so dull and heavy, were as soft and redolent as a song when they touched her. They could give voice to the most urgent, most painful desires, they could send waves crashing to the shores of her heart without a breath of wind. He held her tightly in his arms, suffocating, stifling, yet she wished this moment could last forever.

I love you. I've loved you since you were eighteen. Blood and tears oozed from his words.

Since you love me, what are we waiting for?

Some things are hard to say, some are hard to do.

You looked at your watch. Are you going?

I didn't say anything when I left.

Since you no longer love her, why are you afraid?

I, I don't know. He bent over and kissed away her tears, kissed away the dampness in her heart. I love you. You don't know how much I love you. Moved by his own words, he reached out with his ten magical fingers and touched her again. She wanted to respond, but her heart was like a magnet that had lost its power, cold and hard. He kissed her, kissed her again, releasing a mist of intoxication from a heart whose myriad flowers had lost their petals. She opened her eyes, waiting for the long dark night to end and for something glorious to happen beyond her control. As the warm rays of the early morning sun brought cold, crisp air toward her, she felt suddenly ashamed and resentful of this hostile, destructive love.

I want to see him, right this minute! If I don't, the earth will stop turning, the sun will hide in its mother's womb and refuse to come out. Before she could change her mind, she ran flustered over to his house. Her heart was thumping wildly as she raised her hand to knock. Two steps backward, then one step forward, backward again . . .

The door opened on a family of three like a melody, like a painting, with smiling faces like a melody, like a painting. They walked out into the gold and silver threads of morning sunlight. A breath of cold air rose from the bottom of her heart; she was like ashes like smoke like a clear pond with no fish like fish with no net.

Baobao kiss Papa, say bye-bye!

Baobao, do as Mama says, bye-bye!

A dazzlingly pale little mouth placed a kiss on the scowling face with a golden red backdrop, a sunlit painting. She gazed hungrily at his face, eager to find a flaw, even a slight droop in his eyelids or a wrinkle in his brow. Nothing. She held on to his gaze, the last thread connecting them as she rode off on the bus. Suddenly she felt that love was a myth, like a game played between the angels and the devil, one of life's moist, dry myths. She felt her own love spilling out in all directions, foolish and inferior. She began to pity and despise herself.

The patient's blood pressure is unstable. She's awake. The mouth of her uterus has dilated four centimeters.

You go home, Doctor Ai. Here, use my umbrella. There's no light where you turn at the morgue. It's spooky.

That shows how young you are.

From the conversation between the doctors changing shifts, she knew she was more or less conscious. The night was dark, it was raining, she was on an i.v. She was lying peacefully behind the pale yellow moon, looking down on two arms strapped to a small wooden plank; so much time

51

passed that a pair of ants began moving through her veins. A blunt needle was stuck at an angle in her right arm, but there was no pain, and her heart was empty.

A series of uterine contractions; beads of sweat glistened on her forehead. The pains were like a stone with sharp points tangled up in her heart grinding her guts rocking toward the dark shore over there. Five years ago, on a dark, pain-filled night like this, she had also felt she couldn't put her feet on the ground. But the exhaustion of two days and nights of travel vanished when she saw that familiar face, wreathed in smiles, in the clean, well-lit, medical institute classroom.

Hello . . .

He saw her. He was nervous, flustered. He sneaked her into a small hotel room, where he hemmed and hawed, embarrassment written all over his face.

Say what you have to . . . Holding her fear in check, she tried to put him at ease with feigned calmness.

My studies are nearly over, and I'll be staying in the city, while you'll still be in the countryside. We'll have life-style problems as time passes. Besides, one of the female students is in love with me . . .

She gripped the sides of the bed, her bare feet stepping on thorns in a rose garden. Crystalline drops of evening dew seeped into her wound; she clenched her teeth, refusing to shout.

I'm sorry, don't feel bad . . .

Large, glistening tears crept slowly down her face. She looked at her calloused hands and asked him softly, Why didn't you tell me earlier? Why did you want to be with me the last time you were sent down to the village?

I wanted to tell you, but I couldn't get the words out.

She stood up. He put his hands on her shoulders to help her, but she pushed them away. What bus was she on? Where was she going? She didn't know. She sat in a daze, staring at the lengthening silhouette of a man as it merged with the confusion of the road. A dazzling signboard, "Maternity Hospital," flashed past the window of the bus. She awoke as from a dream, recalling how happy she'd been

52

before she found him.

Which pregnancy is this one? Two big eyes that had never been washed with tears looked out from above a white surgical mask.

First one? Why don't you want it? Illegitimate? Contempt and loathing filled the big eyes.

Because . . .

Because he's married, because he was just having fun with you. He never wanted you in the first place! Women like you, humph!

She raised her head. Tears formed by shame and indignation dotted the mesh, like a fisherman's net pulled out of the water, glistening and shiny.

The big eyes dulled suddenly, indecision; then they bathed her puffy face with gentleness.

You're nearly full term. If you're divorced or something, you can still keep the child, can't you?

She shook her head; the cascading tears were light yellow. The baby isn't a love child.

Oh, so you're looking for the real thing, is that it? The big eyes blazed with color in a sea of ivory.

Go pay and sign in. You take the responsibility for any complications. Next!

She walked through a room filled with deep, dark stares, then entered another room filled with deep, dark stares. Her body was turned into a sieve by the piercing stares, covered with tiny holes into which cold blasts of wind seeped. The stares were crawling with ants; she was a moth-eaten piece of old wood, ready to crumble into dust at the slightest touch. She lay down on the delivery table, a long sheet of white paper, devoid of contents, its end nowhere in sight. A machine began to whir, a sound like bones being ground. She pressed her lips tightly shut, refusing to let screams of pain emerge from her throat. She stared at the ceiling without moving a muscle. For the first time in her life, she was aware of that thin line between life and death, now determined by the movements of the doctor. One minute longer, a tiny bit more pressure, and she would step over that line. A tiny skeleton fell into a pan, making a loud, tinny sound. On sheer reflex she sat up abruptly and looked around.

Lie down, hurry up and lie down! That's dangerous! The lustrous big eyes grew dull and exhausted, as though they had just finished reading the thick book of life. The machine whirred again, and she dimly noticed that the area around the big eyes was dark and clouded, covered with sweat. Her mind went blank, and she knew nothing of what happened after that. A winter passed, maybe a lifetime. She opened her eyes. The room was as bright as daylight; the darkness outside was boundless. She struggled to her feet, but the pain in her belly doubled her up.

Feeling better? The big eyes were isolated between the whiteness of a cap and a surgical mask.

More abdominal pains. She hung her head, not daring to breathe.

Get some rest. I'm an intern. I'm supposed to stay here with you.

Thank you.

Who's coming to get you?

She shook her head and wiped the dried tears off her face.

Wait another five minutes, and I'll have my boyfriend take you home.

She scrutinized those big eyes, feeling suddenly nervous for some reason. After a long moment, she asked, Your first love?

The big eyes quivered slightly. They looked dazed.

She straightened up and staggered out of the maternity ward.

Ai! Ai! Wait a minute . . .

She didn't stop. The big eyes, which had just learned how to veil themselves, watched her disappear behind the curtain of night.

The patient's calm. The mouth of her uterus isn't completely dilated yet.

That's strange. That foreigner's still standing at the hospital gate.

What foreigner? Probably some crazy man from Xinjiang!

No, he speaks English. He said he wants to see his son.

Maybe he really *is* crazy. See his son? You don't suppose

this pregnant woman had anything to do with him, do you?

See his son. A cold gloomy wind found its way through the sievelike holes formed by all the stares, penetrated her skin and bored into the marrow of her bones. She walked alone into the milky morning mist, her arms and legs moving like a mannequin's. She dialed the number and said excitedly, Let's get married. There's nothing but life between us. I have some surprising news for you. She went over to his place the next day, where the green door was opened by a little blonde-haired, blue-eyed woman. She was stunned; her heart grew heavy. Though they'd asked each other no questions, certain looks were both a responsibility and a promise.

The little woman looked at her condescendingly, a clumsy attempt.

Do you want U.S. dollars, or shall I go to the hospital with you?

She looked at the little woman as though she were watching a performance.

My husband went to buy airplane tickets. We're going to leave this place forever.

She pushed away the hand clutching the U.S. dollars and touched the little woman's chin tenderly. Does your husband like to watch these performances of yours? she asked with a smile.

She cast aside her anger and walked away from the little woman. She never went to see him again. She was insulted, she was angry, but she couldn't believe that he'd actually betray that dawn as brilliant as the crow of a rooster. At the very spot where they'd first met, also at dusk, beneath the very same tree, she saw him! He held her hand. The blue gaze in his eyes was filled with the anxiety of desperately wanting to say something. She put her hand to his lips; her heavy, bulging body pressed down on him. The fullness of her breasts and the light movements of the tiny life in her belly made it impossible for her to control her excitement.

I knew I'd find you here.

He cupped her face in his hands. The dignity of the Orient flashed in the blue pupils.

I trust you.

Finding her trust or sincerity unbearable, he masked the inexpressible torment in his heart by kissing her long and hard.

You've suffered a lot because of the baby . . .

It was love that brought me this baby, for which I thank you.

No, oh no, you must let me help you.

You can choose a name.

He wanted to cry, but the tears would not come. He wanted to say something, but didn't know where to begin. He laid his head on her bulging belly and listened blindly for a long time. He was deeply moved by the weak sounds of amniotic fluid flowing inside. It's a boy! he said. A boy for sure. You Chinese all like sons.

What's his name?

Little Dragon. This is the year of the dragon.

A real China hand, aren't you! She laughed loudly, and the miseries of nine months of pregnancy and the burden of insults and rumors evaporated with this first burst of bright laughter. No more words passed between them as they snuggled up and looked at each other. The deepening shades of dusk descended gently behind them like a curtain. They kissed good-bye just as the sun disappeared.

She took a slip of paper out of her pocket. The few lines of crooked Chinese characters bored their way into her soul like snakes: The first time I saw you I figured you were one of those women who goes around sleeping with foreigners. And when you told me you were pregnant, I figured you wanted to leave China and were trying to trick me into marriage. My girlfriend confronted you the other day, and now I know you're a good woman. I want to propose to you . . . the words grew fuzzy until all she could see were shifting rings of light strung together. Lies! People's hearts are so far apart! She stood by the river, its surface like a mirror, looking down at her bulging belly, a bleak ancient tomb, plundered long ago. She was feeling sorry for this tiny life when a cheap lie crept into her mind: she was feeling sorry for herself for stubbornly pursuing an empty dream. She lay weakly down on the cold damp ground and looked up at the icy stars in the sky from nightfall to sunrise.

The mouth of her uterus is contracting. Hurry, get the forceps ready.

Someone shook her head and nudged her face; someone was asking her questions. She wanted them to leave her alone. There was no more blood to lose; her breathing was irregular, but her body was like the wriggling, severed head of a snake that has swallowed a frog. A damp heat came at her from all directions and amassed inside her head, expanding until her skull was about to burst. She raised her puffy face and looked around at nothing in particular. Who was pushing her? She didn't know, but it felt like the hand of death, shoving her faster and faster toward oblivion. She took a deep breath, her body shriveled up into a ball, all the joints creaked noisily.

Push down! Push along with the doctor!

Her head was up against the wall, her face ghostly white; a bone-shattering shriek tore through her larynx. She was about to explode, her whole body felt like a terrorized world! Her breath, her blood, her energy, all spent, leaving only a mass of cooked flesh and blood piled up on the delivery table. Rising steam showed that there was still life in her body. After three days and two nights of depression, with fetal waste clogging up her passages, a tiny old man's face, streaked with the blood of death, bored its way out of her used-up body. She dimly saw the baby's red hair, like a raging inferno. Her heart nearly stopped; she couldn't breathe. A large hand smacked the pale soles of two tiny feet, and the baby chortled loudly. Shivers ran down everyone's spine; they buzzed excitedly, Why isn't the baby crying, why is it laughing? Boundless darkness, a wave of commotion, groups of uneasy people huddled in every corner. The chief internist, the head of pediatrics, everyone was asking why he laughed instead of cried. She wanted to explain to the huddled masses of uneasy people about the lies of conception and why Red Hair didn't cry. But she didn't have the strength, and her lips were stuck tightly together. Her heart was strung up high with an old, extremely thin rope; the slightest movement would send it splattering to the floor. She was like a sick bird perched on

57

the branch of a dead and rotting tree as she listened to the ugly insults and abusive curses coming from all those mouths. Blood and filth snaked down the inside of her legs. She tried to grab herself like an eel, but failed. She crumpled to the floor. This is how it was meant to turn out. She began to cry, she sighed, she nonchalantly cast off the used-up body on the delivery table—let it bleed, let it die. She floated up into the air like a cloud and watched the gaggle of toothless old women rush into the delivery room to drag out the discarded, living corpse, then flew into the pitch black forest. For the first time ever, a rose-colored moon ray appeared in the forest. She stood next to the corpse, not yet rigid, and watched the toothless old women as they fought to strip away the piece of dead and rotting bark (if it exists, we'll call it love). Tiring of this morbid game, she looked underneath her corpse and discovered a nest of dark maggots scuttling back and forth. She found a truth in their midst—he was that gaggle of toothless old women. He and he and he were like a gaggle of frightened toads crouching on the floor, holding a burial rite for love. An old man whose white beard scraped the floor stood behind them chanting an antediluvian drink-ing song that sounded like a curse: the stick hits the tiger eats the chicken swallows the bug bores though the stick . . . the toads began dancing to the drinking song, their movements fast and jerky, their pointed rumps poking holes in the wet mud. She gathered up all the strength she'd had throughout her life and kicked him, burying her pointed toes deeply in his flesh. They came together and formed a whole, sliding down the golden red, grassy knoll into the abyss.

If you love someone you become that person's slave.

Someone in love is consigned to hell.

The pale sounds were caught between his chest and hers, pressed closely together. Frightened, she let him go and ran away, ran until dawn, only to discover that she was still on that same golden red, grassy knoll. A gaggle of identical old women asked in unison if she wanted that piece of old bark. Their smiles were identical, devoid of meaning and vigor, nothing but an expression called smile.

Do you want it?

She stared blankly at the multitude of slobbering chins, longing to rip them all off.

Do you want it?

She took to her heels, ran all the way to winter, ran all the way to snow. Columns of light, sometimes long, sometimes short, leapt amid the silvery snowlight. A tiny building made of silver appeared and disappeared among the columns of light. She walked toward it, but no matter how hard she tried, she couldn't get inside. Looking past the columns of light, she saw that the building was filled to overflowing with large, brightly colored pieces of wood connected by prisms that radiated all the colors of the rainbow. Two children were moving about in an empty space like balls of white cotton.

I know that girl! She shouted, That's a picture of me in my grannie's lap! The photograph had yellowed and was folded, leaving a snowy white scar across her right eye.

Pregnant woman! Hey, pregnant woman!

Quick, a heart stimulant!

She couldn't hear the shouts as she crumpled to the snowy ground in front of the tiny building. Her dim gaze fell upon the girl's greedy little mouth. The girl was staring at a cookie in the boy's hand. She swallowed her saliva and licked her bright red lips.

I'll bet it's sweet?

It is. An orange taste.

The boy put the cookie up to the girl's mouth, then quickly pulled it back.

Let's pretend we're in a movie, okay?

Okay, I'll be the daddy, you be the mommy. Let's kiss.

Disgusting!

We can hide behind that board so the grown-ups can't see us.

Okay. Can I have a little bite?

The girl licked her moist red lips and walked over behind the brightly colored board with the boy. Her breath and blood suddenly froze, like the surface of water with no wind, as clear as a mirror. Off in the distance she dimly saw a forest with no trees, the air stiflingly thick; the absence of everything had become unbearably heavy, she couldn't see the fingers on her outstretched hand, eyes were by now useless, her heart opened up memories she'd never had . . . a silver thread snaked its way out of her heart, like a rope stretching over to the dim opposite shore. Without a moment's hesitation, she slid down it as a voice emerged from the gloom: She's dead!

Four burly men in black clothes black caps black masks picked her graceful ice-cold corpse up with eight big hands covered with bulging blue veins and put it into a large metal box, then pushed it into the fire chamber of a raging furnace. He and he and he and he stood around it watching indifferently as the red flames enveloped the metal box; she stretched out, she curled up, she began to scorch, she was turned into cinders.

They dragged the metal box out of the furnace and opened it noisily. A living organ was squirming amid the cinders.

The four burly men were momentarily frozen solid; their stiffened eyes opened wide as they stared at the organ, unable to move. His and his and his and his eyes met; the floor was covered with frost and ice. A moment passed, then the silence was shattered by a scream, and someone shoved the metal box back into the lovely, inviting furnace with his foot.

A minute passed, ten minutes . . . the furnace hummed, the eyes of the four burly men reddened. Sweat stains on their black clothes formed a hideous design. His and his and his and his face turned pale; their gloomy hearts struck the furnace violently.

The metal box was dragged out again, but before it was opened, the room was flooded with a pale green luminescence.

Amid the pile of white cinders, the living organ was still squirming . . .

RED IVY

1

A GRAY REINFORCED-CONCRETE WALL ROSE BEFORE me like a ferocious tiger, unmoved by the tearful partings and heartrending sobs on either side. Coils of rusty barbed wire covered the top of the wall, evoking a sense of gloom that seemed to hold a macabre attraction for passersby. They stared at it as they walked by, especially the spoiled young maidens and beloved wives, innocent souls used to affection; they contemplated the frightening things that must exist beyond the wall, the dirt and chaos . . . but what about the criminals inside, those who had suffered all their lives? In that prison world, where there were no freedom and no male companionship, were they like women everywhere, arguing over petty matters and becoming enraged with jealousy when they saw younger, prettier women?

After I'd parked my bike, a fat warder came waddling toward me. She had the fleshy voluptuousness of a middle-aged woman, and all I could think of was how wonderfully soft and springy she'd look in the bath. But when she got close, she scrutinized me with an unscrupulous look in her eyes, and an expression spread across her face that people associate with proper, sexless women; it suddenly seemed to me that her spirit was like a towel that had been wrung dry.

She greeted me loudly, as though we were miles apart: "Comrade Ji Li?" She had the heavy accent of a northern peasant, which made her appear simple and reliable. When she shook my hand, it was like holding a potato fresh from the oven. I nodded and said yes. She grasped my hand and shook it hard. "Welcome, welcome! The section chief called to say you'd reported for duty. I'm Liu Yuhua, head of Group Six. You'll work for me." I nodded and said I understood.

"We've got a thousand criminals here, divided into two brigades, six groups, and eighteen teams . . ." Group Leader Liu reeled off the prison organization from memory. "You've been assigned to Team One as its leader. Stay close to me till you know the ropes."

"I'm going to be a team leader?" I pulled my hand out of her grasp, feeling suddenly suspicious that there was more to this official welcome than met the eye.

She laughed easily. "Shit, we group leaders are shorthanded. One of the team leaders was recently assigned to the Discipline Section. Everybody who works for a group leader is also a 'leader.' But still at the bottom of the totem pole." While she was talking to me, she thrust her hands into the pockets of her baggy uniform pants and stuck them straight out. A flat, incredibly broad rump lurched into view as she performed an about-face, spinning on her left foot and stopping squarely in front of me. With a directness that had a tinge of mischief, she said, "I know your uncle's Secretary Li of the Provincial Committee, but you won't catch me kissing up to you. Still, a nice connection like that can come in handy someday." Her unmistakable hint embarrassed me. "Let's go, I'll show you around." With solemn airs, Group Leader Liu became my boss.

On the reddish purple weather-beaten gate, the paint was peeling. It was kept closed the year round to keep the prisoners from getting out. A smaller door to the right was monitored by guards in a metal cage in front, from where they watched all entering guards like hawks.

Group Leader Liu went into the cage and said something to the two guards inside, then signaled for me to go in.

The yard behind the high wall was filled with nesting trees and flower beds, not what I'd expected in a women's prison. But once my gaze landed on the towering plastered walls on all four sides, topped with rusting barbed wire, the fragrant flowers and verdant trees immediately lost their appeal, the air no longer seemed so clean and fresh, and the green lawns seemed to wither and turn blood red. Did these criminals destroy the beauty of society and create flaws in it, or were they the products of a flawed society? In life, with all its yardsticks, anyone whose desires exceed the norm or who momentarily loses control over her emotions may be judged wanting by these yardsticks and become one of society's criminals. And once you are labeled a "criminal," you become a subhuman, stripped of your liberty and your dignity. Remorse and the causes of your crimes become utterly meaningless. Maybe when first offenders walk through this door for the first time, they experience sudden psychological, physiological, ideological, even behavioral changes or a change in their basic nature. Maybe they suddenly see the error of their ways, maybe they feel ashamed and bitterly remorseful, and maybe they say to hell with it all.

"This is the warning line. Prisoners aren't permitted to cross it," Group Leader Liu said as she pointed to a red line painted on the ground a couple of meters inside the gate. The feeling of depression I'd experienced as I walked into the yard as a new guard was quickly replaced by curiosity. I stepped on the line where freedom ended.

"Her name's Huang Li. She's in for murder. A trustee," Group Leader Liu said to me matter-of-factly after we had crossed the warning line. I looked up to see a headful of thick black hair. I quickly lowered my eyes and moved closer to Group Leader Liu, struck by a fear that the murderess might whip out a weapon of some sort.

"Huang Li!" Group Leader Liu called out casually.

"Yo," Huang Li replied in an aging voice that didn't reveal her sex.

I raised my eyes again, with some trepidation, and scrutinized the little old lady in front of Group Leader Liu. Her tiny body was clothed in a brand-new black prison uniform. It was almost impossible to spot her eyes in that pale, wrinkled face. Was this five-foot-tall woman, so frail that a breeze would knock her over, a murderess? With doubting eyes I gazed at the black hair that seemed so out of place on a woman her age. It was as though a lifetime of misfortune were represented in this thick black hair. My presumption disturbed me, since there was no scientific reason she shouldn't have hair like that. It reminded me of the afternoon I had passed by a mortuary and seen two children in white mourning clothes playing house on the stone steps as a column of dark smoke rose in the sky from the crematorium behind them . . . an inauspicious omen, I had thought, though I couldn't say why. Then a few days later, my mother-in-law took ill and died, and I was immediately reminded of what I'd seen on that late afternoon. I was vaguely conscious of a premonition, an inauspicious premonition.

"Put your things together and take them to the train station to be sent home. Get a pass from Team Leader Zhao. Tell her it's my orders and she won't give you any trouble." She sounded superior when she spoke to the prisoner. Maybe she was abused at home, and her occupation gave her a chance to vent her frustrations. Since I obviously didn't understand what this was all about, she cleared things up for me. "Prisoners who were here before 1960 are to be released, but she's been transferred so many times that the records of her conviction and sentencing have been lost. And she can't remember anything about the case. Her two witnesses died of starvation in the sixties, and no one knows the whereabouts of the prosecutor, so no determination is possible. But since her stomach ulcer flared up again recently, the authorities have given her permission to seek treatment outside. They're releasing her to her home. She leaves on tonight's 10:30 train." The way Group Leader Liu described the situation, it was clear she thought Huang Li was getting off lightly. But I was thinking, what if her original conviction had been a mistake? Who was going to pay for the twenty-seven years she'd spent in prison? Sadness crept into my heart, and not just because of Huang Li.

"Bong——bong——bong——" Three muffled chimes from a clock somewhere; the sound lingered annoyingly in the air for a long time. Group Leader Liu told me that was a signal to the cadres from the dining hall. In five minutes the doors would be closed, and even the devil himself wouldn't be admitted after that.

The sound of the chimes still hung in the air as Group Leader Liu took me into the prisoners' dining hall. The first group of prisoners was already at the tables eating breakfast, and when they saw us walk in, they put down their bowls and chopsticks and stood up respectfully. Group Leader Liu took a pudgy hand out of her pocket and signaled for them to sit down and continue eating. They looked at me out of the corners of their eyes. They were eating buns stuffed with vegetables and bowls of coarse rice. "Isn't there enough polished rice to go around?" I asked Group Leader Liu.

Several of the convicts fought to answer: "We have meat every day, good food and plenty of it." Like a prepared speech, in unison and without hesitation. I nearly smiled, but I knew this wasn't the time or place. Lying and saying what you thought your superior wanted to hear had become a habit that had even penetrated the prison.

"Knock that off! She's no inspector from upstairs!" The critical tone in Group Leader Liu's voice was, more than anything else, a reminder to the convicts to choose the proper time to lie. They smiled broadly, and even that was intended to please Group Leader Liu. We left the dining hall and walked over to the head of a stairway. "Isn't there enough polished rice to go around?" I repeated.

"Not enough? They've got more than we have!" Group Leader Liu had thrust her pudgy hands back into her pockets at some time or another, and now she took them out and waved them in front of me. "They have to eat coarse rice once in a while to get a taste of what it's like to undergo remolding. The women in here are a nasty lot, and if we don't make it hard on them once in a while, they'll think they're living in a hotel!" Remolding prisoners isn't the same as sending them to Siberia, but sometimes it doesn't hurt to get tough with them. I couldn't fault what Group Leader Liu was saying, but she sounded more like a nanny than anything else. Yet even though it disgusted me, I nodded in agreement, which probably showed that the demon of hypocrisy had already insinuated itself into my nature.

"There's an amateur cultural troupe upstairs. Three prisoners in our group are members. One of your team's prisoners plays the violin, and they'd do anything to get her to join. But she won't." Group Leader Liu's tone alternated between smugness and disappointment.

The upstairs floor was one big hall with a pile of stuff in the middle of the floor, including some lamps and lanterns, a few guitars, and a broken-down dulcimer. A dozen or so prisoners in red sweatsuits (I couldn't tell their sex just by looking) were standing with their backs to the wall behind a woman who was pleading tearfully to the empty hall:

"You can cast me aside, but I can't cast aside my child."

. . .

"You won't let a prisoner keep her child, but prisoners are people, too!"

. . .

"You've stripped me of my civil rights, but I still have rights as a mother."

. . .

"No, don't leave, let me see my child one more time." She began to wail pitifully, then slumped to the floor.

"Oh, they're rehearsing a play. What about the other role?" I had a pretty good idea, but wasn't sure.

"The prisoner who's playing her husband rehearses in the men's prison," the deputy director of the troupe explained solicitously.

"How can there be any emotional exchange that way? What's the purpose?" I asked.

"If the men and women rehearsed together, it'd be a little too, you know . . ." Group Leader Liu put plenty of feeling into the "you know," so her meaning wouldn't be lost. Once again I was struck by the image of a nanny.

"Why can't men and women prisoners be together?" I asked, feigning innocence. I knew, but I wanted them to think I was naive and artless.

"Those men never see a woman, and if we let them come over and mix with the women, well . . . They rehearse separately, then they get together over New Year's or some other holiday for the actual performance." Group Leader was particularly demonstrative in front of the women, and even though she was just stating the facts, her tone of disapproval was unmistakable. But the women showed obvious interest in the matter, and talked about it excitedly. I understood. It was food for the soul.

66

"Have a seat, Group Leader Liu." Three of the women brought stools over, while the rest of them were less than enthusiastic. I assumed that those three were under Group Leader Liu's supervision. These women knew what was good for them.

"Is Li Zhenzi coming or not? The troupe leader went out to buy her a violin. You've got a lot of talent in your group!" The deputy director of the troupe would go to any length to please Group Leader Liu.

"Enough of that kiss-up talk. I know you want to get into the TV college, and you will if you're qualified. If not, you can kiss up all you want, but it won't do you any good." Group Leader Liu patted the deputy director's shoulder and laughed. By now the prisoners were used to Group Leader Liu's veiled hints.

"Show Team Leader Ji your new dance," Group Leader Liu ordered the deputy troupe director. "She'll understand it."

What made her think I'd understand it? Probably because I was wearing a pair of leotards.

"This is a modern dance. You'll love it," Group Leader Liu said to me.

What made her think I'd love it? I wished I'd changed into the uniform I had been given when I arrived. Group Leader Liu had the wrong impression of me already.

The dozen or so women formed two lines, back to back, their buttocks touching, and stood there motionless. The woman who had collapsed in anguish just a moment earlier was now all smiles. She daintily pushed the start button on a tape deck and said coyly, "Ready, begin!" A staccato, urgent beat burst from the speakers, and I immediately felt as though I had a fish bone caught in my throat, or a case of constipation. Then I realized it was an adaptation of the aria from the Cultural Revolution model opera, *Taking Tiger Mountain by Strategy*, where the hero, Yang Zirong, launches his attack on Tiger Mountain. But this time it was being played on an electronic keyboard and drums. The two rows of buttocks began to sway with the beat, while the rest of the women's bodies remained motionless. After what seemed to be ten minutes, the two lines were facing one another, one swaying to the left, the other to the right, as they gradually merged together in slow gyrations. Group Leader Liu's comment that I'd love it made me uneasy. In the city, whenever a woman is considered "modern," it means she's either immoral or has psychological problems.

"Clerk Chen in the Discipline Section showed us this dance. She even knows how to do the 'Moon Walk.'" Group Leader Liu whispered in my ear, her tiny eyes never leaving the gyrating buttocks of the dancers.

When the song ended, the buttocks stopped swaying.

"What's that dance called?" I asked politely.

"'The Party Is My Mother,'" the deputy troupe director recited. I nearly laughed out loud. Group Leader Liu mistakenly thought my smile meant I'd enjoyed the dance, and she told them to dance another. I hastily asked her to show me solitary confinement.

The right side of the first floor of the cellblock was a row of six individual empty cells about four square meters in size, with bare walls and locked doors and light sockets outside, so the prisoners couldn't stick their fingers into them. The cells were very dark. The guard on duty, named Wu, was sitting in the office across from the cells reading a book. She nodded as we walked in, then went back to her book.

"Reading on duty! Don't you care if your pay gets docked?" Group Leader Liu asked as she hit the book with her hand.

Guard Wu ostentatiously laid the book down and said in measured tones, "Instead of bossing us around, why don't you get a cat and abuse it for a change?"

That did not make Group Leader Liu happy, but she quickly changed the subject. "Any new prisoners in solitary confinement today?"

"Nope. But there's a condemned prisoner in cell six. She's Prisoner Number One."

"A condemned prisoner?" I blurted out, hardly able to believe my ears.

"Yeah, a love murder. A middle-school teacher. Her old man was carrying on with another woman and driving his wife crazy. In a fit of anger she poisoned him and his girl-friend. He died and the girlfriend's a cripple for life. She tried to kill herself but didn't make it, and they sentenced her to death."

"You mean there are still people with such strong feelings?" I said.

Ignoring my comment, Guard Wu continued, "She's scheduled to be shot today at noon. Deputy Warden Zhang was just here." She reached out and pushed a grimy guard log on the table toward me. I opened it up with a shaky hand, beginning to wish I hadn't chosen this profession.

I read the last two entries:

May 12, fair turning to cloudy
Prisoner Number One activities: Stayed in bed all day, didn't eat, said nothing; no visitors.
Requests: None.

May 13, drizzle turning to fair
Prisoner Number One activities: Slept well at night, up at 7:00 A.M., washed up and combed her hair, then lay in bed. Deputy Warden Zhang came to check on her at 9:00 A.M., asked if the prisoner had any last requests; prisoner shook her head.
Requests: Wants to hear tape of violin version of "The Butterfly Lovers" before being executed. Deputy Warden Zhang sent someone out to buy a copy, but he came back empty-handed.

"I've got one." I closed the log and looked at my watch. It was exactly eleven o'clock. "I'll go home and get it, okay?" For some reason I pitied this woman who knew she was about to die.

Group Leader Liu hesitated for a moment, but gave her approval. I ran to the bicycle shed, jumped onto my bike, and headed for home. I forgot that I'd lent the tape to my cousin until I was in my doorway, and there wasn't time to ride over to her house. Suddenly I had an idea. I went downstairs and knocked at the door of the chairwoman of the Municipal

Musicians Association. When this new neighbor of mine, to whom I'd barely said hello, heard my frantic knocking, she rushed to the door without even putting in her false teeth, opened it, and stared at me uncomprehendingly, her hollow cheeks twitching slightly. I flashed a big smile that any actress would have been proud of—even though I hated women who took advantage of their "femininity," I wasn't above doing it myself from time to time. This time it worked, as I could see in the old woman's face. She went back inside and returned with a stack of good-quality tapes. She put on her reading glasses and pulled out one and examined it, front and back, a couple of times before handing it to me. Like an actress anxious to leave the stage, I let the curtain drop as I turned and walked off without changing my expression. It was 11:50 A.M. when I entered the prison, pushing my bike after having snapped the chain because it was so worn out. My heart sank.

I went straight to solitary confinement, tape in hand, to cell number six. The door was ajar, and the scene I saw stopped me in my tracks. The condemned prisoner was sitting cross-legged on the bed, dressed in a neat prison uniform. She sat there in a trance, her clouded eyes no longer seeing this world, but staring straight ahead at the blank wall. It was as though her soul had already departed to be with her husband, leaving behind only a human shell. Another prisoner, a withered little woman in a dark blue prison uniform, was standing in the corner, her eyes blending with the other features on her slack, unhealthy, down-covered face—no tears, no pain. The strains of what sounded like a stringed instrument lingered at the corners of her slightly parted lips, the tragic melody of a lover's yearnings, tearful and accusing, like no other rendition I'd ever heard. There was no passion in the tune, no coloring; each note was a withered vine or a dead tree standing in the midst of a snowy landscape, exposed and vulnerable to the wanton abuse of freezing winds. Liang Shanbo and Zhu Yingtai were meeting not in a tower, but in a remote, uninhabited region north of the Great Wall. This woman was already dead, at least her heart was. Group Leader Liu was also in the cell, a look of anguish on her face.

The refrain was repeated, and I thought that maybe this melody, which sanctified the frolicking of the butterflies in a fairyland, would bring comfort to the two women. But no. The song was a disturbing one, evoking the feeling of an autumn wind sweeping across a cluttered grave site, or a rainstorm turning a well-traveled path into a sea of mud. The condemned woman, her peace shattered, was standing at the window, her face deathly pale, without a trace of color. I felt like crying, and I wondered why people did this to themselves when they were about to die. I stood there in utter silence.

The clock tolled three times, long and drawn out, and my first thought was that in five minutes the dining hall door would be closed. I'd gotten up late that morning and had had to hurry to report in on time, so I was hungry. Then I'd spent nearly an hour pedaling back and forth on my bike on an empty stomach. Group Leader Liu glanced at her watch. Probably as hungry as I was. There'd be no more peace of mind for either of us now. We must have looked at our watches ten times in the next minute. And I began to suspect the genuineness of my heavy feelings of a moment earlier. Maybe because I'd had such a pleasant childhood I didn't know how to relate to the suffering of others. Or maybe it had something to do with the way the condemned woman had been singing the refrain of "The Butterfly Lovers," or maybe just because she was numbed by impending death. Those feelings of mine had been nothing more than petty bourgeois sentimentalism! As I turned to leave, I nearly bumped into two armed guards from the execution party . . . white uniforms, white caps, white gloves, two enormous white objects flashing past my eyes . . . my heart contracted, and I was having trouble breathing.

The condemned prisoner was taken away. Police vehicles were parked in front of the cellblock, red as blood, their sirens silent.

2

THE FIRST THING UNCLE DID WHEN HE RETURNED FROM his provincial inspection tour of sixteen factories in ten cities was meet with various specialists and professors. He picked their brains like someone attacking a milk shake with a straw, soaking up every precious drop of wisdom, the fermentation of years of blood, sweat, and tears. These brains, filled to painful capacity, willingly gave up their nourishment to Uncle, who drained it easily and stored it up for his own use. These wise people were trading their knowledge for wealth and position, for the opportunity to enroll their children in proper day-care centers, for improved professional status, for better and more spacious housing, and for all sorts of commodities. Of course, what we're talking about here is sleight of hand, not public exchanges.

My fraternal cousin, who had a stack of rejected manuscripts almost as tall as herself, detested these opportunistic, fawning men and women who used my uncle's office and position to get their nondescript writings into print, which turned their authors into pseudosensations. But she detested even more her inability to cash in on her own talents. Having missed her chance to attend college, she was now too old. The thought of taking a graduate entrance exam had occurred to her, but she was afraid the rampant pretentiousness of institutes of higher learning would bring an end to the comforts and pleasures she'd enjoyed all her life; of course, that might have been a smoke screen to mask her fear that she'd fail the exam.

Once, on a whim, she had sat for an exam, and when she read the classical Chinese section, with all those pedantic expressions and vague allusions, she didn't know whether to laugh or cry. She couldn't answer a single question and didn't feel like trying. With a smug look in her eyes, she glanced around the room, filled with backs hunched over like so many little humpbacked bridges, and laughed over how ridiculous it was to sweat over all those dead allusions. She tossed down her blank examination booklet and strode out of the hall, her head held high, her chest thrown out, feeling more superior and self-assured than if she'd turned in a perfect paper. She stepped through the door with a sense of transcendence: washing windows, cleaning toilets, boiling water for tea, and emptying spittoons at the guesthouse where she worked was no more boring than useless research on the birthplace of one of China's famous novelists or determining the semantic difference between "unity" and "collusion." At the guesthouse, every guest, Chinese or foreign, scientist or peasant, relied upon her for boiled drinking water, information on mealtimes and a supply of bathing water. She was fond of saying that value equated with necessity. But that was nonsense! Toilet paper and astronauts are both necessities, but are they of equal value? She'd look at those semiliterate girls (if written words were four ounces apiece, they couldn't manage a pound's worth) who came to work wearing glass-beaded necklaces and gaudy synthetic dresses, their permed hair stacked up on their heads like pug dogs, their lips painted as if they'd been eating raw, bloody pork, and who stupidly stuck out their rumps and thrust out their chests around young men as a sign of their blossoming sexuality, then started each day by flushing twenty-two toilets, cleaning twenty-four spittoons (there were two in the corridor), putting covers on twenty-two TV sets, and laying out twenty-two pairs of slippers, and she'd feel like picking up an ashtray and flinging it at someone's head—it didn't matter whose. But she never did. The girls feared and respected her as a cultured woman who'd leave the guesthouse someday and make a name for herself. They came to her with their problems, big and small, especially for help with their love letters, in search of a fashionable new term. And no matter how disgusting their requests were, she always forced herself to be patient, to see what it was like to be considered broad-minded and magnanimous. After the girls had left, she'd glance over at the clock on the desk, whose little hand had moved up another notch, and grumble between clenched teeth, "There goes another hour of cleaning toilets!" There'd been no time for writing lately, for after leaving home in the morning, she was too busy rushing about in the company of foreigners and famous

Chinese. "A" introduced her to "B," from whom she heard about "C" . . . A-B-C-D, what a small world; by now she knew them all! It didn't take her long to weave a net—not a fishnet, but a human one. She mocked all her would-be suitors, who couldn't communicate on her level; she mocked the friends and relatives who tried to fix her up, and showed no respect for her privacy; and she mocked all those stupid people who sold their souls for college diplomas. She had a new pet phrase: "When you deal with people at my elevated level, sparks fly!" (I teased her once by commenting, "Watch out you don't burn up!") And so, even though she had a stack of rejected manuscripts almost as tall as herself, her grand personal reputation preceded that of her writings. A certain Swiss sinologist had asked her to photocopy some Tongcheng County gazetteers; a professor of philosophy from the University of Kansas had asked her for an introduction to a deep-breathing specialist at the provincial hospital; the Hong Kong magazine *The Intellectual* was going to publish her far-ranging conversations with American friends; the Beijing magazine *The Orient* had asked her to polish a piece sent to them by a reader . . . my cousin's wisdom and talent had become public knowledge, and everyone who knew her felt ennobled, even though fame had thus far eluded her. Simply stated, my cousin had become the head-rope of a vast net.

Yesterday she had come to see me to set up an appointment with my uncle. I'm fully aware of how insignificant poets and writers have become in my uncle's eyes, especially now that his interest in literary activities has waned and in the wake of last year's frenzy of association meetings. The provincial chapters of the Writers Association, the Folk Literature Association, the Dramatists Association . . . they all welcomed him enthusiastically into their chambers, but the doors were too low for someone like him, and he felt nothing but contempt. So he took all his fancy membership cards and tossed them into Auntie's metal button box. But that didn't deter him from his desire to see my cousin, whose grand personal reputation had thus far preceded her writings. That was partly due to his eagerness to discover new talent, but also because she was, after all, my cousin.

As I led her into the house, we were met by the crisp, resounding laughter of my uncle in the living room. What wonderful laughter! As though it came straight from his diaphragm and was funneled through a long copper tube, producing the same effect as viewing the brilliant rays of the morning sun. Mother had once told me that no matter how hard I cried as a child, the mere sound of Uncle's laughter was enough to turn my cries into loud laughter. We walked into the living room, where our eyes were drawn to Uncle's bright, shiny forehead, which seemed to illuminate the whole room, and his powerful jaw. His eyes were bright yet calm; his bearing was unrestrained yet solemn. He was leaning back on the sofa, engaged in a discussion with a group of balding scholars. He acknowledged our entrance with his eyes without pausing in his discussion. In a genial, yet unmistakably patronizing tone, he turned to a scholar beside him, a man with a gaunt face and heavy jowls, and asked him, "How's that article of yours, 'Population and Employment in the Year 2000' coming along?"

I was surprised to learn that Uncle's tastes had expanded to matters of national interest, but I tried not to show it. The old scholar pulled a few strands of white hair from his right sideburn all the way across his bald pate and casually picked up a notebook, which he held out as far as his arms would allow, and looked at it for a moment. "I've finished the third section of chapter four. It should be done by the end of the month."

Uncle grunted loudly, then turned until he was leaning across the armrest of the sofa next to the old scholar with the gaunt face and heavy jowls, so he could face an old woman wearing thick glasses. "You're the women's rights expert. Did you finish your study on the status of China's women?"

The frail old woman deliberated for a moment, then said stiffly, "Yes." During the long pause that followed, Uncle kept his eyes fixed on her to make her continue without any help from him. "Owing to current political, economic, cultural, geographic, and ethnic factors," she went on in a squeaky voice, "the majority of China's women are resigned to their oppressed status. A minority of educated urban women have

75

elevated their consciousness to the point where they have rising expectations about equality, independence, clothing and makeup, love, marriage, family, even sex, but their outside environment has changed very little. Since they're still surrounded by a feudalistic society, they're restless, anguished, and uneasy. The gender gap is so great that many women still view men as the source of strength and love upon which they rely. But owing to ethnic degeneration and years of constraints—the outside pressures on men are greater than on women, because of their job assignments—Chinese men are in a state of desperation. There doesn't seem to be any chance in today's society that someone will take up the struggle for women, and spend the time and energy to get the job done. For men, of course, this represents a measure of progress."

Uncle's neck was getting sore, so he straightened up and leaned back on the sofa. He took out a notebook, as if he were going to make some notes; but he didn't write anything after all, leaving the impression that he was just putting on a show of respect.

"In a word China's women are in the position of seeking the historical status achieved by men!" My cousin, unable to hold back any longer, stood up and interrupted the old woman, whose only response was to let her mouth fall slack. Like a teacher criticizing one of her students' papers, my cousin had summed up all that gibberish in one terse sentence. She walked to the center of the room, one hand on her hip, the other waving in the air, as she continued emotionally, "Women in China may get equal pay for equal work and they may enjoy economic and social independence, but society is still dominated and controlled by men. If this continues, women will be nothing more than accessories, like a blouse, a flower, a home, or a token female at the head table. They're viewed as important and indispensable only because they produce sons and give men life's greatest pleasure. A long history of subservience and slavery under the deep-seated colonial mentality of men has instilled in their consciousness a sense of spiritual and emotional dependence. They're like a rudderless boat, unable to steer itself to the shore, never realizing that the shore they seek doesn't exist in the real world, unless, of course, they themselves are that shore.

"Yet what women yearn for is the love and protection of men, and to achieve it they let themselves be spoiled and appear weak. Take sex, for example. Most people are ignorant in matters of sex. Women's sexuality is suppressed. Young women frequently flaunt their ability to resist an attraction to young men, and married women don't actively seek their own pleasure. Some women even take pride in an indifference to sex to show how proper and morally upright they are. This mentality of using a diaper as some sort of fashionable scarf is a real tragedy. And look at all those men who are sexually impotent—to them this natural bodily function only dissipates their manliness. Some men no sooner climb out of bed than they dig around for a tonic of replenishment. That kind of ignorance and selfishness is a blasphemy against human nature. Neither men nor women have the guts to say what they want, nor fully enjoy what they have every right to enjoy. They twist sex, which is decent and good, into an ugly monster. But that being said, we need to take a hard look at the true state of our economic and domestic environment. Generally speaking, after a man and his wife get off work at night, they squeeze onto a crowded bus to get home, where they have to do the washing and cooking, and look after their children, all in one tiny room. And since inflation has made buying food for the family a major problem, how can they be expected to think of any sort of enjoyment?"

The words flowed from her mouth like a river, and her monologue on sex had the old scholars utterly stupefied. Yet they sat there without blinking, looking intently serious so as to preserve their Confucian gentlemanly demeanor. Properly benign expressions adorned their faces. They relaxed a bit as my cousin paused to drink some water. The old woman, whose glasses were as thick as the bottoms of pop bottles, shook her head disapprovingly to show her contempt for my cousin's absurd theories, while the others began discussing other topics among themselves to show that her comments were not worthy of their time.

77

But she was too caught up in her monologue to worry about outside interference, and the chilly reception merely served to enhance her eloquence. When she had finished the water, she coughed loudly to regain their attention and force them to listen to what she had to say. She was still standing in the center of the room as she picked up where she'd left off: "I recommend that the provincial League of Women set up a women's club to give our women a chance to get involved in a host of activities. The goal would be to balance their state of mind and improve their natural qualities. There could be a variety of activities, and they could choose the ones that appealed to them. Here are some I've thought of: We could have a room where aesthetics and psychology are discussed, and we'd invite experts in these fields to lecture them on feminine psychology and aesthetics, like how to preserve their feminine beauty and charm and how to slow down the aging process—physical and mental. This could be expanded to include lectures on how middle-aged women can keep their figures, how older women can make themselves up discreetly, how young women can use their natural beauty to best advantage, how to keep their bellies from sagging, how to get rid of crow's feet and facial wrinkles, and things like that. Another room could be reserved for external matters. We could have experts talk about government affairs, home management, managing time, or the lives of important women, past and present, Chinese and foreign, plus things like how women can protect their economic and emotional independence, and how they can become self-reliant and avoid the torment that comes with losing someone you love. This could open their minds and their eyes and improve their ability to compete in society, at home, in their marriages, and in affairs of the heart. It could make them invincible.

"The third room could be called the grievance room. Any woman who couldn't vent her grievances at work, at home, or wherever, could do it here. The room would be equipped with plenty of breakable things, just waiting to be smashed. And you could even order a replica of someone you hated, which you could hit, kick, or tear to shreds. Or you could go into a soundproof room, where you'd lie down on a plush

green carpet and scream or shout or cry your eyes out. All
you'd have to do is say the word, and for next to nothing you
could get it out of your system. That way it wouldn't fester
inside and affect your physical and mental health, and you
could avoid taking your frustrations out on others in society
at large or at home.

"The fourth room could be the meditation room. A small,
absolutely quiet room equipped with a bed and nothing else,
pitch black, so only your thoughts would be active. You could
think about someone or something, you could reflect on
aspects of your life, or you could relive parts of it. The fifth
room, if permission could be obtained, would be the ren-
dezvous room, where lovers could meet happily and without
nervousness under circumstances of total safety and secrecy.
That way they wouldn't have to go around sneaking kisses.
Of course, it mustn't be construed as an opportunity to
commit adultery." Her spontaneous exposition took me com-
pletely by surprise. In preparation for seeing Uncle, she had
spent a lot of time planning not only what she was going to
talk about, but even what to wear. On our way over she'd
seemed paler than usual, her lips redder than usual, but not as
though she'd used face powder or lipstick. Then I looked
more closely and discovered she had used face powder and
lipstick, but then had wiped most of it off, leaving just a trace
to give the illusion of natural color. I had never realized she
knew so much about makeup. Unfortunately she had decided
to wear a pair of tight jeans with a high crotch to make her
legs look longer, with the result that one of her low-slung
buttocks was stuffed into the left pant leg and the other into
the right, which only accentuated her typically Chinese figure
with its long waist and short legs. She stood in the middle of
the room, legs apart, anxiously bemoaning the state of women
everywhere. Her presence, her bearing, seemed to fill the
room. As she spoke, her eyes grew misty and she began to
appear transcendent, as though she were the only person on
earth, and it was up to her to create the human species out of
clay, a race of men and women infused with her will and her
emotions; she would be humanity's redeemer.

Even Uncle was awed by her presence. His eyes were fixed

79

on her, his mouth hung open motionlessly; he had the dazed look of someone who wanted to speak but couldn't, yet was unable to comprehend what he was hearing. His usual unrestrained demeanor had vanished. The gaunt-faced, heavy-jowled old man and the woman in the thick glasses sat frozen in their seats, completely under her spell. Cousin was more alert and resourceful than most people, and she knew when it was time to stop. She'd once said that one must never try to tame a man completely, especially in front of others, because one day he'd realize what had happened, and his ego would force him to detest the woman who had tamed him; he'd never be able to love her again. So when she realized that the critical moment had arrived when her listeners were ready to get off the subject, like lawmakers about to pass a new bill, she walked up beside me and led me upstairs to see Auntie.

When we entered Auntie's bedroom, she was bending over picking matchsticks up off the carpet. I knelt down to help her, but she pushed my hand away. "What's going on?" I asked. "Wouldn't it be easier to kneel down and pick them up instead of bending over like that?"

Auntie ignored me and finished picking up the matchsticks, then wiped her sweaty brow. As though she had discovered one of life's universal truths, she said with joy and satisfaction, "Twenty is better than twenty-five. I can pick them up seven times without getting light-headed, and stretch my spine and tighten my abdominal muscles just right." She tossed the matchsticks back down onto the carpet. Twenty red-tipped matchsticks lay where they fell on the dark green carpet.

I was more puzzled than ever. I took a good look at my aunt's slim figure, noticing that her belly was as flat as a board. "You don't have an ounce of fat down there!" I exclaimed.

"Ah, so it was you holding forth downstairs a moment ago! Sit down," she said to my cousin, ignoring my comment as she finished picking up the matchsticks and sat down in an easy chair.

My cousin merely smiled in response.

Then my aunt turned to me and said, "Your uncle's been

eating out so much these past few months he's developed a real potbelly. In the States, a man with a potbelly lacks that competitive edge and has trouble finding work. And I want you to know that there may be a change in your uncle's position . . ." The tail end of her comment broke off in her throat. I knew that was because my cousin was in the room. Apparently sensing the impropriety of stopping in midsentence like that, she patted me on the shoulder, as though she were petting a kitten, and said, "Now don't you go saying anything about this."

Cousin sneered at Auntie and said in a solicitous tone, "You were a top pupil at Beijing Medical College, so why were you in such a hurry to leave? All you worry about is your husband. What about yourself?" Cousin was an expert at knowing what to say and when to say it. With her caustic tongue, she could drive a point home even when she was ostensibly praising or commiserating with someone.

Her comment cut Auntie deeply. She froze for a moment, but quickly regained her equilibrium, picked up a sweater she was knitting, and said, "You youngsters don't understand people of my generation. I like to recall something my mother-in-law told me: she said that girls are like seedlings. Wherever you plant them they grow. And, of course, a woman takes a husband for richer or poorer."

"Your mother-in-law was illiterate, and she had one child after another. Your father-in-law became an official right after liberation, so being a wife and mother was her only option. But what about you, a talented physician?"

"I gave life to five fewer human beings than she did, all in exchange for the ability to write the word person and nothing more." The gentle tone of her voice could not disguise the sarcasm.

"But because you have the ability to write the word person, you should know that the relationship between a man and a woman must be based on equality." Combative by nature, Cousin forgot herself in the heat of battle.

"Aren't he and I equal?" Auntie's voice was more gentle and tranquil than ever, yet there was an unmistakable note of scorn in her tone. "Isn't harmony the same as equality?"

"No, it's not!" Cousin fired back, her head thrust out in front of her.

"Can men and women ever be equal? Take menstruation, for example. Is that a result of incomplete evolution or simple proof that men and women are just different?" Auntie was getting spirited. This was the first time she'd talked with anyone like this in years. "Except for when she's going through the physical and emotional trials of pregnancy, lactation, lying in, menstrual interruptions, or menopause, the average woman spends seven years of her life menstruating! If you add all those other years together, when a woman's body is unbalanced and her mood keeps fluctuating, you can imagine the incredible toll it takes on her strength and health, and all this during the most precious years of her life. Time and evolution have made men strong and women weak. Strength and power have been the primary ingredients in the development and triumph of the human species. A patriarchy replaced a matriarchy, and the heavier, more demanding jobs were gradually taken over by men, including those with the highest visibility, like foreign relations, politics, economics, and culture. Women, on the other hand, assumed the lighter, less strenuous tasks of rearing children and other domestic duties. It's a vicious cycle: men have broader vision, are physically strong, and have well-developed intellects, while women are limited in their outlook, parochial, suspicious, clinging, and lacking in relative intellect. Of course, men aren't our equals in things like patience and tenacity. In the struggle for existence, men naturally play the dominant role. Since women have been under male domination for so long, the only way they can assure themselves of long-lasting love and the protection of men is to be obedient, conciliatory, self-deprecating, and ingratiating. In China especially, with its thousands of years of history, the standards by which women are judged are determined by men, based upon their sense of beauty, their interests, and their needs. Our dear Confucius summed it all up in his three obediences and four virtues. So our poor grandmothers and their mothers before them were forced to strap down their breasts and bind their feet, they weren't allowed to set foot outside the house, they weren't to show their teeth when they laughed or open their mouths when they ate, and they were cursed and reviled for having girls instead of boys. If their husbands died when they were still young girls, they couldn't remarry . . . the psychological residue of thousands of years has entered our genes and has been transmitted from generation to generation, one on the heels of another for centuries. And that's made it next to impossible for us to achieve equality with men. So . . ."

"So you're content to be dominated. But since it's residue, as you say, it must be changed. The pace of change in the status of women has increased astonishingly fast! Look at Madame Curie, Empress Wu Zetian, even the fashionable Mrs. Thatcher. In China we have equal pay for equal work, divorced women can take custody of their children, unmarried women can get abortions, bras have become ornamental attire . . . if I'd talked like this in the twenties, my only choice would have been between suicide and being buried alive."

"But don't forget that when Mrs. Thatcher leaves the political scene to return to private life, she'll revert to the role of taking care of her husband and children, just like a servant! And if an unmarried woman gets an abortion, the child's father can just walk away and leave her with a stain she'll carry for the rest of her life."

Uncle came upstairs to get a notebook just then, bringing the war of words between my aunt and my cousin to an end. Auntie lowered her head and went on with her knitting, casting glances at my uncle and my cousin out of the corner of her eye. Cousin, who pretended she hadn't seen Uncle enter the room, picked up Auntie's ball of yarn and said softly, "Hm, pure wool, and a popular color."

"Um, he bought it for me when he was in the States last year. He couldn't wait to spend a few dollars on me." She said it casually, but her meaning was clear to me.

"This color will go beautifully with your fair skin. You're not even forty-five yet, are you?" A question pregnant with hidden meaning.

"Forty-seven. Getting old. How about you? Thirty-seven, aren't you?" Even more hidden meaning in Auntie's reply.

83

"Uh-huh. I was born at the end of the year, so by Chinese reckoning, I'm two years older."

"Time to think about taking care of things, isn't it? What about that artist Ji Li introduced you to? The one labeled a rightist for twenty years."

"That's over."

"Over? Didn't he say you'd moved into his studio last year? I thought you two got married." There was a slightly malicious tone in Auntie's voice.

"That shameless pig! I figured he was going around spreading rumors!" Cousin erupted like a coiled spring.

"What good would spreading rumors like that do him?" Auntie asked casually.

"They don't do him any good, but what they do to me . . ." Cousin stopped abruptly, cursing herself for falling into Auntie's trap.

After digging through a pile of books for a while, Uncle finally pulled out a dog-eared notebook. He opened it and read aloud, "In 1963 there was an average of 8.5 square feet of housing space for every person in the province. In 1976 that number shrank to 3.4 . . ." He closed the notebook, turned to us and said excitedly, "This is it, this is the one!" He walked out, seemingly oblivious to the bitter verbal contest between my cousin and my aunt. Could he have been completely unaware that he'd been the cause of that conversation?

3

THE DRIZZLING RAIN WAS LIKE A MIST. RATHER THAN OPEN her umbrella, Huang Li let the misty rain fall on her. Her pale face was so wrinkled that the water spread out and merged from one channel to the next instead of dripping straight down, turning her deeply creased face into a shifting sheet of moisture, until it looked like a spongy goatskin that had been soaked in water. True, if you looked hard enough, you could discover a tiny pair of blinking, rheumy eyes tucked in among the creases of her brow.

The asphalt road was covered with a film of rain, like the

filthy sweat on a deeply tanned back. It was a sight she often saw: her husband's back turned to her as he sneaked a bowl of gruel he'd brought back from the dining hall. Huge, wet parasol leaves stuck to the road. They reminded her of the urine stains on her bedcover. Water-filled potholes in the road amid the leaves reflected the branches overhead. Leaf and branch, one real, the other illusory, one true, the other false, gave her the feeling that walking along this road wasn't really going home.

"Who wants to go back to that foul-smelling house?" was what she was thinking, although her feet kept taking her forward, like a runaway old machine.

"Roasted yams! Two kilos for one yuan!" A peddler was shouting from inside his stall on the street corner.

Two kilos for only one yuan? How could they be so cheap! Huang Li thought back to the famine, just before she had been sent to prison, when they sold for ten or twenty yuan a half kilo. She rushed into the stall. "I'll buy them all!" she said, panting, "All of them!"

The old moon-faced yam peddler raised his head and gazed at the sun-starved face in front of him, wreathed in thick black hair. His mouth fell open as if he'd seen a ghost, and he couldn't say a word.

She took off her black prison jacket, tied the sleeves together, scooped up all the yams, roasted and raw, in and around the oven, and dumped them into the jacket. Taking ten yuan out of her pocket, she stuffed it into the hand of the stupefied old man, then turned and ran outside. When he saw her rush off like an escaping convict, he was dumbstruck. Then he looked at the ten-yuan note in his hand and realized she had change coming. He rushed out of the stall and ran after her. "Hey, come back!" he shouted. "Come back here!"

The shouts only made her run faster; looking straight ahead, she darted right and left until she reached a place she thought was safe, where she sat down to catch her breath. When she looked down at her cache of yams, she congratulated herself on the terrific deal she'd made. But as she stood up, the sleeve of her jacket came loose, spilling the yams onto the ground. She dashed around picking them up out of the mud.

"Hey, there's a big one over here, Grannie . . ." A little freckle-faced girl was holding a yam in her hand as she stared at Huang Li's pitch black hair and unbelievably pale face, a prison legacy. She ran over and hid behind her mother. Just as Huang Li reached out to take the yam, she quickly drew her hand back in fright.

"Little Huahua," Huang Li mumbled, "Little Huahua."

"My name's not Little Huahua. It's Little Ling," the girl said timidly from behind her mother.

But Huang Li kept mumbling "Little Huahua" as she turned and walked away.

Famine.

Her little room was pitch black, like a mausoleum, where darkness accompanied the loneliness of death.

A sound in the corner, the rumbling of an empty stomach, then movement. She got up and walked outside, where it was as dark as it was inside; she thought she could see the road beneath her feet as it twisted and turned down to the wheatfield at the bend in the river. It was the wheatfield, all right; she could feel the wheat in her hands. After picking a wheat stalk, she blew away the chaff, stuffed the kernels into her mouth, and began to chew. Another stalk followed. The husks and beards she couldn't spit out went down with the rest. And so it went, pick, rub, chew, until she was so tired she was panting and sweating.

Village women are the biggest gossips in the world. Whenever someone brings a girl or a new wife into the village, her life is scrutinized from every angle. Talk leads to sympathetic sighs and, ultimately, to insults and abuse. At first they curse her behind her back, but when that loses its appeal, they begin saying things to her face. But all she can do is bow her head and pretend they're talking about someone else: "People take advantage of the weak and fear the strong, don't they?" She must console herself.

"Oh, didn't you know! She's married to the stammerer in our village. Poor thing."

"Here she comes. When she stands upwind, you can smell

her piss odor a mile away!"

"Look at her hair, like pig bristles! And black as a scorched pot!"

"In the village we say that decent people don't have hair like that! And we normal folk know what we're talking about."

"She's got a mole under her right eyelid. That's a sign of somebody who starts by gaining the upper hand over her parents-in-law, then does the same to her own parents."

"Since she did nothing good in her previous life, now she's getting what she deserves. Four pregnancies, four breech births—not one of them lived. Now she can't keep from wetting and messing her pants."

"That only happens if you do you-know-what when you're pregnant."

"Tsk-tsk."

"She can't even stand around other people. Her pants are always wet, and she has to wear one of those napkins all the time. Her crotch is covered with urine sores, so itchy they drive her crazy, and if she scratches, her fingers are covered with blood."

"Tsk-tsk."

"She's no good! A woman with no shame is like a tree with no bark. She keeps standing upwind and won't go away!"

"Was her man disgusted with her?"

"You bet he was. He wouldn't even climb into her bed. The year before last he rolled up his bedding and took up with the widow from the Liu family in the village up ahead. He never set foot in his house again. Look, there she goes."

"That scummy, half-dead old widow! Not an ounce of shame!"

"That's right. A woman shamed is worse than a dog. A man shamed just ups and leaves."

"Does she eat in the big dining hall or the little one?"

"How can she eat in the big one if she doesn't work in the fields? She's lucky to get a couple of bowls of rice gruel and half a hunk of steamed bark and bread. And that bastard the stammerer used to fetch her food for her, then eat it himself!"

"How does she survive?"

"They say that every night . . ." The gossipy woman stopped before she'd finished and swallowed the rest of her sentence as she broke out in a cold sweat. Back then, who would have been bold enough to mention the word "adultery"?

"Adultery? Beat her! Then see if she does it again! No answer? Pull down her pants, string her up, beat her!" The field supervisor picked up a willow branch and handed it to one of the men.

After her thick black braids were tied together along with her hands, she was strung up on the roof beam. The field supervisor reached up and jerked her pants down. A foul-smelling napkin fell at his feet. Urine dripped down her thin, bony legs to the floor. He hit her as hard as he could with the switch, then walked off holding his nose, leaving the rest of the beating to the others.

There didn't seem to be an ounce of flesh on her bones. Her ribs stuck out like venetian blinds, and her belly seemed to bump smack up against her spine; her thin, bony legs hung limply down and swayed gently. She looked like a skeleton wrapped in a yellow sheath. Her underpants were so shredded by the willow switch they no longer covered her genitals. Only a few drops of blood oozed out of her torn flesh and quickly congealed as she hung there wide-eyed without making a sound, as though the willow switch were flailing someone else.

Another torrent of urine dripped down her legs, and the man waiting to beat her with the switch threw it down and ran off.

Her little room was pitch black, like a mausoleum, where darkness accompanied the loneliness of death. She forced her eyes open, but couldn't see a thing. She had no idea when she'd been taken down and laid out on her brick bed or how long she'd slept. Her head was splitting, and her chest felt as heavy as if it were being crushed by a huge boulder. Where were her hands? Where were her legs? She tried to force her senses to the surface by rolling over. One of her arms lolled over the edge of the bed; now, at least, she knew where it was. She bent her head over as far as it would go and licked the back of her hand, then bit it. The pain brought her to her senses. After pushing herself up into a reclining position with the hand that had some feeling in it, she slid off the bed onto the floor. With all the strength she could muster, she managed to get up on her hands and knees. After wiping the sweat from her brow, she reached under the bed and pulled out a staff, using it to climb unsteadily to her feet. Then she headed off toward the wheatfield at the bend in the river with mincing steps, as though she were running, or floating in the air, or carried along on a wave.

The sun was up. Seeing her lying face down in the marshy wheatfield, her mouth caked with mud, the field supervisor kicked her several times, waking her up, then dragged her back home and tossed her into the room. No one ever saw her outside again.

Something shocking had occurred! Word spread through the village that she'd killed freckle-faced Little Huahua, the daughter of her neighbor, the field supervisor. Little Huahua was his sixth and last child; her mother had died in childbirth. Since he was busy night and day watching the fields, all the food sent over from the small dining hall, plus the barley he was able to steal, wound up in the stomachs of the older kids, leaving nothing for Little Huahua. All day long she crawled on the floor looking for crumbs. Before long even that was impossible, and her body began to bloat. She curled up in front of Huang Li's door and lay there all day.

Little Huahua's father looked for two days without finding a trace of her. Then someone told him she'd seen Huang Li drag Little Huahua into her room, and she hadn't come out again. Someone else reported hearing screams and wails coming from the room a couple of days earlier.

That night the field supervisor brought the militia and forced his way into the room. It was so dark inside he couldn't see a thing, but a powerful stench of urine nearly bowled him over. He flicked on his flashlight and stumbled fearfully back to the doorway.

She was sitting in the middle of the room, her hair hanging

89

loose, holding the stiff body of Little Huahua in her arms . . .

A couple of days later, two members of the security force came over, cuffed her wrists, and led her away. From the day she entered prison, she had food to eat and water to drink, and even though it was never quite enough, she was eternally grateful. The investigation and sentencing went off without a hitch: she pled guilty to all charges. On the day she entered prison, she was given a new name by the county Public Security Bureau: Huang Li. Her husband's family name was Huang, her maiden name Li. This was the custom in that locale, so she didn't object.

"Huang Li, stop right there!" An apricot yellow motorbike pulled up beside her.

Huang Li took a step backward, let her arms fall to her sides, and bowed her head, the prescribed position for someone being reprimanded.

"Ha, ha." Jiang Hong, who was sitting on the motorbike, laughed so hard her breasts jiggled. She jumped off the motorbike and put her hand on Huang Li's shoulder. "Just look at you! I knew I'd scare the hell out of you if I tried to sound like Group Leader Liu." She unconsciously swayed her ample hips alluringly as she spoke, casting sexy glances at some boys who were standing nearby gawking at her. It had the desired effect on them. She stretched her arms languorously and smiled radiantly; a woman displaying her feminine charms for all to see. One of the boys screwed up his courage and walked up to her, pretending to ask directions: "How do you get to the train station?" She looked into his eyes until he nearly took leave of his senses. "That way, then turn to the right," she said as she pointed down the street; a thick wallet disappeared into the purse at her waist. She smiled, and he smiled back as he walked off.

Jiang Hong turned back to Huang Li, who had already left the scene. She ran up and caught her. "You old reprobate, old Jiang Hong here is going to take you to her house and pay you back for what I did to you in prison."

Huang Li tried to get away.

"Is that any way to show your appreciation? Listen here. I

heard you were getting out today, so I took the day off. Wow! What are you doing with all those yams? Have you gone crazy?" She wrenched the yams out of Huang Li's hand and dumped them into a trash can. Then she started up the motorbike before Huang Li could react, put her arms around the old woman's waist, and deposited her on the back of the motorbike. She climbed onto the seat and said, "Hold onto my waist, close your eyes, and sit still, or else you'll be splattered all over the street, you old bumpkin!"

Under normal circumstances, Huang Li moved more slowly than Jiang Hong, but now she was so frightened she could barely move at all. She took in a gulp of cold air, wrapped her arms around Jiang Hong's bulging waist, and screamed, "Don't go! Stop!"

"If I hear another word from you, I'll drive it straight into the wall and finish you off!" That was all she had to say. In prison Jiang Hong had taken advantage of her so often that Huang Li was deathly afraid of her.

Even after the motorbike had come to a complete stop, Huang Li was still holding onto Jiang Hong's waist for dear life. Jiang Hong pried her fingers loose, climbed off the motorbike, lifted Huang Li off the passenger seat, and deposited her solidly on the sidewalk. But Huang Li, unsteady on her feet, fell smack down on the ground, and began throwing up violently.

"You old bumpkin, haven't you ever taken a ride before?"

"They took me to prison in a car," Huang Li said between retches.

"Ha!" Jiang Hong doubled up with laughter. "You've wasted an entire lifetime! But today I'll give you a taste of the good life!" Jiang Hong dragged her into the building and up a flight of twisting stairs to the second floor, where she pushed her into her room. Huang Li bowed her head out of habit as she surveyed the contents of the room with tiny eyes hidden in the creases of her face, like Liu Laolao when she first set foot in the mansion of *Dream of the Red Chamber.*

"Get out of those prison clothes!" Jiang Hong ripped the black holiday prison jacket off Huang Li, then took a dark blue wool jacket from a pile of colorful clothes in the corner and helped her put it on. "I picked this out just for you!" she said, demonstrating with two fingers how she'd picked it out.

Huang Li didn't know what to do with her hands. Jiang Hong rolled the prison jacket into a ball and tossed it into the garbage pail behind the door. Huang Li stole a look behind the door as she fiddled with the new jacket she was wearing.

"Sit down. There on the sofa. Group Leader Liu has one of those in her office. Sit down, why don't you? Lost your senses again?"

Huang Li sat down on the edge, but her rear end had barely touched the seat when Jiang Hong took her hand and led her over to her bed. "Lie down and try it out. It's a Simmons. It's what foreigners sleep on. I've been to Group Leader Liu's house. She's got a wooden bedframe tied together with ropes and a comforter full of holes where the kids have wet the bed."

Huang Li didn't want to get up on the mattress.

"Didn't you have surgery to cure your leakage problem? So why not try it out?" Jiang Hong picked her up and sat her on the edge of the bed, then rushed over and turned on the TV. Since there was no daytime programming, the blank screen just crackled. She turned the set off, then went over and switched on the four-speaker stereo tape deck, which immediately flooded the room with the sounds of a tearful ballad. The music made Huang Li uncomfortable. She looked around. Jiang Hong, anticipating as much, switched it off and dragged Huang Li over to the dining table. She opened the refrigerator and took out four plates of cured meat, which she placed in front of Huang Li, who pushed it away in a panic, as though she couldn't stand too much good fortune.

"You don't eat meat? This is meat, meat!" Jiang Hong, who was accustomed to tormenting people, drew the word "meat" out until it slid off her tongue like glistening fat. All of a sudden, it was as though the only meaningful thing in the world for Huang Li was the food in front of her. She swallowed hard a time or two, then breathed a heavy sigh, as if she wanted to rid her body of everything unrelated to the hunger inside her, emptying herself for all the delicious food in front of her.

Gulp! She swallowed a mouthful of saliva, then took a small medicine bottle out of her undershirt pocket. It was wrapped with sticky gauze. She tore off a small strip and stuck it on her forehead above her right eyelid. A rheumy little eye that had been all but hidden exploded onto the surface of her face.

"Aren't you going to tape open the left one?"

"One eye's enough." With that, she picked up a pair of chopsticks and dug in.

Jiang Hong laughed loudly and walked over to the refrigerator, took out a bottle of beer, and held it up to the window to shake it. Then she smacked the bottom of the bottle with her hand, and the cap flew off with a loud pop, landing on the other side of the door. Huang Li's mouth fell open in fright; a piece of meat fell to the floor. Before Jiang Hong had even noticed, she reached down, picked it up, and stuffed it back in her mouth. Jiang Hong poured a glass of beer, slurped the foam off the top, and handed it to Huang Li. "Here, have a glass."

Huang Li finished off half in one swig without even tasting it. Then she popped another piece of meat into her mouth.

Meanwhile Jiang Hong sat off to the side watching her eat, a sense of contentment rising from the depths of her heart. She didn't want to miss a single motion, especially since everything was happening under her direction.

Huang Li ate like there was no tomorrow, but not sloppily. After every bite of meat, she licked her lips and fingers carefully with her pointy red tongue.

"Don't just eat the pork. Try these mushrooms. They cost five yuan a jar. Raised by hand." Jiang Hong placed the open jar in front of Huang Li, who stuck in her chopsticks before she'd even swallowed the piece of meat in her mouth.

"This is jellyfish, right from the sea, damned expensive!" Jiang Hong held up the plate like a magician and dumped half of it into Huang Li's still full bowl. "Well, my dear, looks like we'll have to make the bowl deeper!"

Huang Li ate and drank so fast it made her head swim, and before long she was belching loudly.

"Ai! In prison I ate your special hospital food twice. Does

this make up for it?" Jiang Hong asked as she picked up a piece of glistening ox tendon between two polished red nails and rubbed it across Huang Li's lips as if she were teasing a cat, then pulled it back.

Huang Li was drinking soup straight from the bowl. "Um," she muttered.

"Don't drink so much soup. I've got desserts you've never seen before." Jiang Hong took the soup bowl out of Huang Li's hand, cleared the table, and held up a tin of fancy sweets.

Huang Li had the will, but not the room. She bit off a piece of peach crisp, but couldn't get it down.

"Don't force it," Jiang Hong said. "You can take them home with you." Without wasting a second, Huang Li put the lid on the tin of sweets and stuffed it into her bag. Her meaning was clear: They're mine now. She stood up with difficulty, then sat back down and swept the bones and food crumbs into a little pile with her hand.

Jiang Hong smiled. "Does this meal make up for the two times I slapped you in prison?"

Huang Li grunted like a sow that had gorged herself.

Jiang Hong laughed loudly. "Would I have had all this if I'd gotten out of the business, like Group Leader Liu said?" She lay down on the bed and stretched out comfortably. "It's worth it," she said emotionally. "Like I haven't had enough to eat? Or I haven't had enough fun? Who else could get a wad like this with one quick move?" She took out the boy's wallet, tossed it up in the air, and caught it. "A day of freedom," she said complacently, "is a day of pleasure. Life's worth living! Feast your eyes on this. See how many men tag along behind me!" She took a stack of color photos out from under her pillow, all of them showing her being held and kissed and hugged by different men. She handed them to Huang Li, who was about to nod off to sleep.

A knock at the door. Jiang Hong shot out of bed, gathered up the photos, and asked affectedly, "Who is it?"

"It's me."

"Oh, Group Leader Liu!" Jiang Hong opened the door, grabbed Group Leader Liu's hand enthusiastically, and said, "Come in, please come in."

Huang Li's sleepiness disappeared at the sound of Group Leader Liu's voice. She stood up, let her arms fall to her sides, bowed her head, and stood in front of Group Leader Liu.

Group Leader Liu silently scrutinized Jiang Hong, walked over to the bed and picked up a photo she'd missed. "True love this time?" she asked.

Jiang Hong didn't dare make a sound. Group Leader Liu's eyes softened suddenly. "When are you two getting married?"

All things have their masters, and plaster of Paris is stronger than bean curd. Knowing she could never lie to Group Leader Liu, Jiang Hong remained speechless for a moment before muttering, "He, he's got a wife . . ."

"You, you . . ." Group Leader forced back what she was going to say. She was sure that Jiang Hong would be back under her supervision one day, but for the moment, at least, she was a free woman.

Group Leader Liu thrust her hands into her pockets and stuck them out as far as they'd go. She took a turn around the room. "From the look of things, you're about to become a three-time loser!"

Jiang Hong looked up and smiled bashfully. Group Leader Liu turned and looked sternly at Huang Li, who had been under her supervision at ten o'clock that very day. "Huang Li!"

"Yo!" Huang Li took a step backward to maintain the proper distance between prisoner and guard.

Group Leader Liu softened and took pity on the woman. "How come you left without your release pass?" she asked as tenderly as she knew how. "The train doesn't leave till ten at night, so what's the hurry? The group was planning to see you off. Why'd you just take off like that? Here, these are your certificates for outside medical treatment, your health records, your baggage receipt, and a letter of introduction to your village brigade." She put the documents into an envelope and handed them to Huang Li. "Now, remember," she said, "when you get off the train, wait at the main exit, and don't move. Someone from your village brigade will be there to meet you. Who knows, maybe your old man'll even be there!"

"Right, right," Huang Li said without raising her head. The creases in her face were twitching, but it was impossible to tell if she was crying or smiling.

"Repeat it for me."

"When I get off the train, I'll just wait there . . ."

Jiang Hong rolled her eyes lightly. "Group Leader Liu," she said solicitously, "I have to meet someone on the ten o'clock train tonight, so I can take her. You've been working hard all day, and you've got kids at home, so I'll take her for you."

"You're really going to the station?" Group Leader Liu asked, even though she knew what was going on.

"Really! Look, I've already bought my platform ticket." Jiang Hong patted her empty jacket pocket.

Group Leader Liu, who had indeed worked hard all day, closed one eye and looked at Jiang Hong with the other, as though she were pleased to accept Jiang Hong's offer. Jiang Hong saw Group Leader Liu out the door, then darted back inside, unable to hold her amusement in any longer, and collapsed on the bed like a dismembered skeleton. "There, I've left the door wide open!" she shouted.

4

TWO RECTANGULAR TABLES AND EIGHT STOOLS IN THE visiting room separated the prisoners from their families, who sat opposite them at the tables. It was the responsibility of the guard at the head of the table to check the visitors' parcels and listen to conversations, and, of course, keep track of the time.

In the morning Team Leader Ji took the drug addict, Li Zhenzi, into the visiting room, where Li's husband, Shi Li, was waiting in the corner of the family reception room on the other side of the wall. He nonchalantly walked over and sat down across from Li Zhenzi, took off his glasses, and cleaned them over and over with a handkerchief. She kept her head lowered the whole time, concentrating on the edge of the table.

Team Leader Ji looked at her watch, either out of concern that they were wasting precious time together, or because she was anxious over whatever it was that Li Zhenzi was feeling deep down in her heart. She stood up, coughed dryly a couple of times as a sign that she was leaving, and walked into the outer room. Not a trace of suspicion or gratitude from Li Zhenzi. Keeping her head lowered, she continued to inspect the edge of the table.

Team Leader Ji took a turn around the room before sitting down. Shi Li went over and picked up a plastic basket from the corner of the room, which he filled with things he'd brought in his backpack. "Two kilos of apples, a box of powdered milk, two bags of sugar, fifteen hard-boiled eggs, and two packages of vitamin C. Exactly two and a half kilos." He placed the filled basket in front of Team Leader Ji for her inspection. She nodded, gave it a quick glance, and put it all into Li Zhenzi's bag.

"The guards treat you better than your own father and mother, so make sure you do what they say . . ." a teary-eyed, gray-haired old woman sitting behind Shi Li said, although it was impossible to tell how genuine her words were.

"Mother, our team's very progressive. We have political study sessions on Mondays, Wednesdays, and Fridays, and on Tuesdays, Thursdays, and Saturdays we have vocational instruction. Everything's just fine, Mother. The guards treat me well, I eat well, my accommodations are fine, the sanitation is fine . . . how's Father?" As a new prisoner, she was just mouthing formalities. But when she asked about her desperately ill father, she laid her head down on the table and cried loudly.

Group Leader Liu, who was sitting at the head of the table fishing around in one of her nostrils with the end of a pencil, said impatiently, "Not so loud. You'll disturb the others!" But it would have been impossible to disturb the others, who were so concerned with taking advantage of each of the forty minutes of visiting time to talk and to cry that they paid no attention to what was going on around them.

"Make sure you don't fight with the girls in your cell, because if there's any more trouble, they'll add another year or two to your sentence. Your father wouldn't be able to hold on long enough to see you again . . ." Tears and snot ran down the old woman's face.

"Mother, isn't Father getting any better?" The young woman's eyes were red from rubbing.

"Don't cry, Chen Xiaocong. Swallow your tears so they'll form a pool of perseverance and stamina inside you! I hate tears! Stop crying! If you can't even control your tears, how are you going to get your criminal behavior under control?" Group Leader Liu saw that Team Leader Ji was watching her as she repeated the same thing she'd been saying since last year, word for word.

But it worked with the young woman, who stopped crying, wiped her nose with her hand, then wiped it dry on the sole of her shoe.

"Time's up. Go on back, Chen Xiaocong," Group Leader Liu said as she made a notation in the log with the pencil with which she'd been fishing around in her nostril.

"All right, Group Leader," the young woman said as she stood up and walked timidly over to the door. But she abruptly turned around and thrust her neck out like a rooster and said, "Ma, when will you be back again?"

The white-haired old lady was walking through the door, crying so hard she couldn't answer.

A look of sympathy spread across Team Leader Ji's face. She looked at her watch and said to Shi Li, "Time's up for you, too."

As though a heavy weight had been lifted from her shoulders, Li Zhenzi raised her head. There was a vacant look in her eyes, as though she were looking at Shi Li but might be looking past him. "Don't come back," she said softly. "Just file the papers."

"Don't talk like that, please don't talk like that," Shi Li said, as though those were the only words in that head of his. He stood up and reached across the table to pat her shoulder. Then, like someone afraid of catching a contagious disease, he retreated into the corner.

Li Zhenzi walked out of the visiting room, her nose running, feeling as if she were about to sneeze. Her legs felt like they were filled with lead and vinegar; they were so heavy, they ached so badly, she could hardly move them. She leaned up against the door of the packing workshop, her head lolling weakly against her chest. A pair of tiny birds flew noisily overhead, chaos reigned in her heart, and she began to tremble. Was this, she wondered, what death was like? A multitude of hands seemed to be reaching out from her heart for something forever beyond their reach. Her mouth tasted terrible and there was a horrible tightness in her chest; the stench of rotting garlic made her feel like throwing up. Thick purple lips, so big, so soft, so foul smelling, so cold . . .

Under the light of the rose-colored oval lamp, the thick, purple lips were like leeches firmly attached to hers. Her stomach was churning and she was about to throw up. Pushing his face away with all her might, she ran out of the office of the leader of the hospital's Dictatorship of the Proletariat team, trembling from head to toe, her knees knocking violently as she ran.

The internal medicine office was flooded with light. Her colleagues, all intellectuals, didn't forget to smile at this troubled colleague of theirs. Everything seemed foreign to her, foreign and frightening.

The elderly head of nurses walked softly up and stood beside her for a long time without saying a word. When they heard the sound of footsteps in the corridor, she said in an affected, grave tone of voice:

"You can go see Shi Li at ten o'clock tonight."

"Oh!" Li Zhenzi gasped, like a hen that's just laid an enormous egg. She blushed.

The head of nurses grasped her hand and stood there a moment longer before turning and walking off.

The offices were unusually quiet, now that the doctors had left for the day. Li Zhenzi sat alone at the end of the sofa, staring blankly at the clock on the wall.

A nonviolent struggle session had commenced at the hospital.

A group of coal diggers in their miners' hats were lined up across from some white-clad doctors and nurses, waving their banners and shouting, "Whoever the enemy opposes, we support. Whoever the enemy supports, we oppose!"

Not to be outdone, someone in a white smock raised a huge megaphone and blared through it, "All reactionaries are paper tigers . . ."

Li Zhenzi walked over to the window. Since night had fallen, all she could see were the lights of the miners' lamps. She was suddenly disoriented. Was she at the bottom of a deep, dark mine? If so, why wasn't she frightened?

"Be resolute, fear no sacrifice, surmount every difficulty to achieve victory! Be——re——so——lute——" The miners in their hard hats were singing in ranks, all the way through at first, then one syllable at a time as they stomped their feet rhythmically.

Li Zhenzi was mesmerized by the scene, until the clock on the wall chimed once. She jerked her head back to look at it, then spun on her heel and ran out.

The streets were chaotic, with people moving all about, pasting up slogans, reading big-character posters, and shouting slogans. Naturally no buses were going anywhere. She knew that Shi Li was locked up in the political study room at the bottled-gas works, a good two kilometers from the hospital. She cut across the street, skirted the wall of Southern Mountain Park, and ran as fast as she could. The tree-lined boulevard was pitch black, no lights anywhere, making it impossible for her to see where she was going. Suddenly, at an intersection she couldn't even see, she heard a chorus of low, raspy male voices that had a mysterious quality in the darkness: "The latest instructions from our Great Leader, our Great Teacher, our Great Commander, our Great Helmsman are to dig tunnels deep, store grain everywhere, never seek hegemony . . ." Li Zhenzi was so frightened her legs turned to rubber. She stumbled and fell against a poplar tree by the roadside, where she held her breath and didn't stir. Not until the singing had faded into the distance did she continue her journey.

When she reached the bottled-gas works, the leader of the Dictatorship of the Proletariat team, the one with the bad breath, was guarding the entrance. He pointed the way for her, and she turned and headed toward a low building standing alone to the right of the compound without so much as looking at him.

Her heart was pounding uncontrollably as she reached out to open the door. But she got a grip on herself before walking inside. She rushed over and put her arms around Shi Li, who was lying on a pile of rushes, without saying a word. She could barely recognize him in the pale light. Shi Li's clouded eyes were nearly closed as he collapsed into her arms. His face, deprived of the glasses he normally wore, was pale and swollen. He was gasping for breath, as though his windpipe were clogged.

Suddenly overcome by a fit of coughing, he broke out in a fine sweat, and began tearing at his collar with both hands as his face darkened and his head swayed back and forth. After a moment he arched his back and began clawing at the skin on his neck, wheezing and coughing so violently he wet his pants. Li Zhenzi was an internist, but she'd never had a patient who coughed like this. Unable to control herself any longer, she began to bawl like a baby.

Shi Li coughed for a long time before gradually quieting down. Now that he'd caught his breath, he spoke fitfully, "Those records of people who died . . . not a question of malpractice. And definitely not a matter of politics . . . bad breath . . . jealous . . . I was the attending physician . . . then there's you . . . keep those records in a safe place . . ." He started coughing again. Spittle with traces of blood oozed out of his mouth and dribbled down his chin.

"Tuberculosis, your tuberculosis has flared up again!" Li Zhenzi said anxiously.

"Time's up!" A teenager dressed in an olive drab uniform and brandishing a red-and-white stick stood menacingly in the doorway.

As though this were their final parting, she grasped his hand tightly.

The teenager walked over with a mean scowl on his face and pried her hand loose with his red-and-white stick. "How can you carry on like that in broad daylight!" he roared. "Get out of here!"

Terrified, Li Zhenzi stood up and Shi Li slumped back down to the floor, his eyelids drooping weakly. Thinking he might have died, she shrieked and called his name. He responded with a weak shake of his head, so slight it was barely noticeable. But it was enough to calm her down. She turned and followed the teenager with his red-and-white stick out the door, utterly dispirited.

When she got back to the hospital, Li Zhenzi sneaked some tuberculosis medicine out of the medicine cabinet and filled half a vial with the tablets, which she planned to give to Shi Li. Then she felt her way in the dark back to the bottled-gas works, but the windows and doors of the room where Shi Li had been kept were thrown open and the room was empty. An elderly woman standing watch at the gate told her that right after she'd left, some men had put Shi Li on a truck and taken him somewhere, but she didn't know where. Li Zhenzi paced back and forth in front of the gate, her mouth dry, her tongue brackish, seeing spots in front of her eyes. She wandered off aimlessly, crying without being aware of it, until she suddenly found herself standing on the bank of the Huai River, listening to the sound of the silver-capped waves, like a suckling baby. Her heart skipped a beat. What impulse had brought her here? Recalling the vial of tablets in her grip, she felt as though she were holding Shi Li's life in her hands. She wished she could plead his case for him, but she realized the futility of that thought. Not knowing what to do, she walked blindly forward, eventually being swallowed up in the deepening darkness.

As dawn began to break, without being fully aware of what she was doing, she knocked on the door of the man with bad breath. The door opened, and a wave of rotting garlic hit her full in the face. Wishing she hadn't come, she wanted to turn and run. But it was too late. The leader of the Dictatorship of the Proletariat team dragged her inside, closed the door, and held it fast with his broad back.

"His . . . his tuberculosis has flared up again, and you know it. This medicine, he needs it right away . . ." Why was she here? What would come of it? She tried not to think too much, but deep down she already knew.

"What medicine is that? Let me see." Before Li Zhenzi could utter a sound in protest, a pair of purple lips, like leeches, were pressing down on her mouth and her tongue was being sucked painfully. She fought to get away, but bad breath was like an aroused tiger, panting lustfully. He wrapped his arms around her waist, picked her up, and threw her onto the bed. Then, with his arms and legs stretched out, he pinned her frail body solidly beneath his huge frame. She stopped resisting, and didn't truly come to her senses until foul-smelling sweat began dripping onto her waxen face.

He was like a deflated ball. With the little strength he had left, he said, "From now on you belong to me."

She felt like a piece of rotten, oozing meat, covered with maggots in the blazing sun, with blue bottleneck flies buzzing in and out of her heart. It's over for me, any chance of happiness gone forever, she thought. At that moment she knew what the future held.

"Why did you have to marry him anyway? Because of you, I had to marry a woman from the countryside, and I go to sleep every night hugging a pillow." Amused by his own comment, he giggled like a baby after feeding time.

She was shocked and frightened by what she'd done. After getting dressed, she held the bottle of tablets, which had been in her hand the whole time, in front of his relaxed, contented face and said, "Let him go."

Choosing not to get dressed, he stood in front of her, stark naked, wrapped his hand around hers, and said with a distressed expression on his face, "It's already gone too far . . ."

"You! . . ." Her heart was beating wildly, but since she couldn't wrench her hand free, she spoke as calmly as she could manage: "He'll die if you don't let him go now." Then her anger took over. She opened her mouth as though she were going to bite him, just for a second, then shouted, "You promised!"

He quickly covered her mouth with his hand and pointed with the other to the window. "Will you promise to come back tomorrow night?" he asked hoarsely.

She pulled her hand back and walked stiffly out the door.

103

Li Zhenzi's throat was burning; a painful fire was raging inside her. She could barely keep from falling down, and her head felt like a medicine ball, heavy and devoid of air. By holding onto the wall, she felt her way to the toilet behind the dining hall, shivering and trembling.

A moment later she floated out of the toilet, a devilish smile on her face. The back of her hand was bleeding from a puncture wound, but instead of going back to work in the workshop, she hid behind a pile of bricks, sitting comfortably up against a poplar tree to soak up the warm rays of the sun, like a stove in the winter or a warm bath in the summer. She was luxuriating in a warm tub while Shi Li massaged her back; he stopped rubbing, his hands poised in the air . . . she felt like singing, or like laughing out loud . . . she could spend the rest of eternity in the golden waters of the tub . . .

She and Shi Li were schoolmates, but not classmates, so they merely said hello to one another. But fate intervened when they were assigned to the same hospital. They traveled together on the train, reported in at the hospital together, received their white smocks and hats together . . . one to internal medicine, the other to surgery, one upstairs, one down, seeing each other going to and coming from work and at mealtimes. On one occasion she left the hospital with her director for a consultation. A few days later she returned, and when they met in the dining hall, Shi Li made a fuss in front of the doctors and nurses lined up to buy lunch, "Where have you been?"

She blushed. They sat down next to each other to eat. "Did you miss me?" she asked softly.

It was his turn to blush. His face was as red as a rooster's cockscomb in the presence of a hen.

Soon afterward, a tall, well-built medical student was assigned to the hospital as chairman of the local Association of Medical Students. A month later he was appointed as party branch secretary of the surgical department. Although weak in basic theory, his technique in abdominal surgery was flawless. He assisted the nurses with injections, changed dressings, brought water for the patients, and emptied bedpans. The way he treated his colleagues was diametrically

104

opposed to Shi Li. There was always an amiable look on the face of one, while a smile never appeared on the face of the other, except for the benefit of Li Zhenzi. Doctors and patients alike were more impressed with him than with Shi Li, but Li Zhenzi considered Shi Li more dependable.

Following a residents' meeting one day, after the branch secretary, who sat behind Li Zhenzi (he never sat at the table), had handed out his instructions and assignments, she discovered a folded piece of paper in her pocket. She opened it and read: "Meet me in the bamboo grove behind the residents' quarters at 2:00 this afternoon." Li Zhenzi understood, but wasn't sure what it was all about. When she arrived at the bamboo grove at two, she saw him waiting beneath a blooming Chinese redbud tree. He spotted her and coughed to catch her attention. "You wanted to talk to me?" she asked with feigned innocence.

"I want to tell you . . ." A wave of garlicky stench hit her full face. Her stomach churned and she took a step backward. She held her breath as she looked at him.

He didn't mince words. "I love you," he declared. The news nearly floored her. "What do you think of me?" he persisted.

"Everyone's more impressed with you than with Shi Li."

"How about you?"

"Sure . . . sure, me, too." Something kept her from saying what was in her heart, but whether it was his powerful physique or something else, she didn't know.

"Honestly?" He drew closer to her and said breathlessly, "I'd treat you better than Shi Li does."

She kept retreating, trying to escape the garlicky stench.

"I truly love you." He drew up right in front of her and took her hand. She pushed him away roughly.

"Why did you do that? Why?"

"You . . . you've got bad breath." She ran off laughing.

He stood beside the redbud tree like a simpleton.

That evening, while they were watching television, she told Shi Li what had happened. No response. But as they were walking later that night, he said through clenched teeth, "What makes him think he can feast on a swan with a foul-smelling mouth like that!" In the dark Li Zhenzi threw herself into his arms, and she could hear him gnashing his teeth.

"Here you are, Li Zhenzi, loafing on the job!" Xu Zifang, the woman who'd murdered her lover, kicked Li Zhenzi in the rump.

Li Zhenzi was staring at the rustling leaves of the poplar tree and making bird noises like a little girl.

"What'd you do to your hand? It's all bloody!" Xu Zifang was staring wide-eyed at the puncture wound on the back of Li's hand.

Li Zhenzi looked up at her and smiled sweetly, then recommenced making bird noises.

This so frightened Xu Zifang that she turned and ran. "She's deranged. Keeps making bird noises, smiling . . ." Xu Zifang reported, almost incoherently.

"Didn't you take her to the medical clinic?" Team Leader Ji asked impatiently.

"Uh-uh."

"What do you mean, uh-uh? All you ever do is report people to impress us." With a parting glare at Xu Zifang, Team Leader Ji ran over to the site of the incident.

After wrapping Li Zhenzi's hand with a handkerchief, Team Leader Ji ordered the hulking, impetuous kidnapper, Chen Dehao, who was standing at the side of the road gaping, to carry Li Zhenzi to the medical clinic.

While the outside doctor was bandaging Li Zhenzi's hand, he grumbled angrily, "Since she has no desire to live, why not just let her die!"

The elderly convict doctor wordlessly handed the outside doctor antiseptic, cotton, and scissors. Once the wound was dressed, the elderly convict doctor cleaned the instruments, then walked softly over to the outside doctor's desk and said to him cautiously, "Someone who wanted to kill herself wouldn't cut small veins like that. Especially an experienced doctor."

"Humph! Do you think someone like her really wants to commit suicide? All she wants to do is scare the hell out of the prison staff." He glared at the elderly convict doctor, who could see that this wasn't the time to say any more, and kept his wrinkled mouth shut. The outside doctor ordered the elderly man to give Li Zhenzi a general examination. After listening to her heart with his stethoscope and prying open her eyelids to check out her pupils, he asked the outside doctor tentatively, "Is she on sedatives?"

"Oh!" Team Leader Ji blurted out. She could have kicked herself for forgetting about Li Zhenzi's history with drugs.

The elderly convict doctor knew he'd guessed right. "Very clever. Since she had the drugs but no syringes, the only way she could get a fix was to cut herself . . ." The elderly man had momentarily forgotten his place as a convict, forgotten the secondary role he was supposed to play, and had pronounced his own diagnosis before giving the outside doctor a chance.

"Impossible! Where could she get drugs?" asked the outside doctor, either out of stubbornness or in order to retain his self-respect.

"Well . . ." This silenced the elderly convict.

Team Leader Ji thought for a moment, then ordered, "Tell the woman on duty at Team One to examine her bedding."

Li Zhenzi was lying on the examination table having her blood pressure taken. Her right arm was puffed up to the size of her thigh under the pressure of the inflatable rubber cuff. The nurse walked out when she was finished. The sun's warm rays shone through the window onto the right side of Li Zhenzi's face. She saw gold flecks in front of her eyes, then silver flecks, crystalline flecks . . . as colorful and beautiful as a river of gold and silver. When she was a little girl, she'd seen a painting in her mother's room of a stream flowing between two mountain ridges, composed solely of the naked bodies of countless infants. The babies were sleeping peacefully, in all sorts of poses, like so many crashing whitecaps, yet somehow tranquil. Golden flecks, silver flecks . . . infant flecks . . .

Something was forced into her mouth. It was a pill. She didn't swallow it right away, preferring to hold it in her mouth for a while to savor its bitter taste.

"Is she okay?" Group Leader Liu, who had rushed right over, asked as she swept into the room.

"She's calmed down a bit since she arrived," Team Leader Ji answered softly from the window.

With a stern look on her face, Group Leader Liu walked up to the sickbed. Li Zhenzi stared up without recognizing her. "We can't save you! You resist remolding, you run away from it, you oppose party discipline and the laws of the land, not to mention the cadres responsible for you, by trying to kill yourself. It looks like the only thing that'll bring you to your senses is a couple of weeks in solitary confinement!" To Group Leader Liu this was an extremely serious matter.

Team Leader Ji, on the other hand, wanted to show how different they were in terms of emotional reaction, so she smiled warmly and lowered her voice as she said, "Not so loud. She's not even completely conscious yet." Even she knew that was not true.

"Telephone, Group Leader Liu," a prison nurse reported.

"You stay here and watch her, Team Leader Ji. I'll relieve you for lunch."

"I had a bowl of instant noodles a little while ago," Team Leader Ji lied, both to show Group Leader Liu how well she could take care of the patient and to keep her from interfering. Two birds with one stone.

"Don't stay too late, then," Group Leader Liu said with concern, to show her appreciation. She shook her flabby arms and left the room.

Team Leader Ji moved a stool next to Li Zhenzi's bed and sat down. For some strange reason, she was feeling nervous, as though she were waiting for something without knowing what that something was.

The sun's rays, having moved across Li Zhenzi's face, were reflecting off one of the lower panes of the window; her face was now cloaked in the misty light of dusk, as waxen and motionless as a mask.

A fly was crawling up the outside of the window, banging into it occasionally, obviously trying to get into the room. After several failed attempts, it flew off, but was soon back to try again, doing everything possible to get inside. Li Zhenzi discovered that Team Leader Ji was as mesmerized by the sight of the fly's futile attempts to reach its goal as she was.

"That day when they brought Shi Li home . . ." The crisp sound of her voice broke the extraordinary silence of the sickroom. It bore little resemblance to Li Zhenzi's normal voice, sounding more like the strange bleatings of a lamb.

Team Leader Ji grew excited, as though the moment she'd been waiting for had suddenly arrived. Wanting to maintain her role as a team leader, she leaned over and asked in a voice that didn't reveal too much concern, "Want some water?"

Li Zhenzi didn't answer. Her eyes seemed to be looking up at Team Leader Ji, but might have been focused on some point behind her. "The look of sincerity in his eyes," she continued, "scared me. I avoided his eyes and lowered my head as I prepared his bath water, then washed his clothes. When he'd finished his bath, he took an empty vial out of his new underwear, the one that had been filled with medicine, to put it in the wooden box that held our valuables, like his diploma, our marriage certificate, and our census registration, as a memento. I guess he was reluctant to put it away, because he just held it in his hand for a long time. 'If you hadn't asked someone to bring this to me, I'd probably have gone to see Karl Marx long ago! I know it sounds funny, but they never beat me again after that day. I wonder who it was who came to my aid. I'd like to thank that person!'

"That scared me even more, and I couldn't even look at him.

"'What's the matter, Zhenzi?' He pulled me close and held my face in his hands.

"I screwed up my courage and told him everything. At first he just shook his head, but then he rested it on the table and stared blankly. I kept perfectly still, not making a sound. He didn't get up from the table until the sun had set outside, when he stumbled into the bathroom and threw the little medicine vial into the toilet and flushed it down. I fell onto the bed. He stayed in the bathroom for a long time before coming over to the bed, where he looked at me for a moment, then walked over and started washing his clothes. Sometime in the middle of the night, he finally came to bed, very cautiously, as though he were afraid of touching me. He pushed my covers up next to me, then lay down with his clothes on. The night was so still I felt like crying, but I didn't dare make a sound, didn't dare move. I just lay there with my eyes closed and listened to the sounds of the wind outside. He might have been asleep, for all I know, but it seemed to me that he spent the whole night glaring at me.

"Some newspaper pasted on the wall in the outer room was blown to the floor by the wind, making a swishing sound. He jumped out of bed without lighting the lamp and stood there barefoot as he shouted, 'Who's there? Who is it?' The mental anguish this caused me was too much to bear. I covered my head with the comforter and started to cry, but he just stood there until the cold was too much for him, then climbed back into bed. For several nights after that, I woke up in the middle of the night coughing and saw him sitting on the edge of the bed smoking a cigarette. I offered him a divorce, but he didn't say anything one way or another. So I didn't mention it again after that.

"He took me to work every evening and picked me up at night. He did the washing, cooked the meals, and for all people knew, he was the ideal husband. He was purer than I was, and more noble. But every day I spent in the shadow of his nominal forgiveness was like a year. What did I owe him? How much? The better he treated me, the greater the pressure I felt. I began to find some solace in morphine, and soon grew addicted to it. Then I started stealing some of my patients' drugs, which led to incidents at the hospital, including the death of a patient. After I was sent to prison, he came to see me every month, rain or shine, bringing me things to eat and other necessities. You know the story after that, but if there's anything else you'd like to know, just ask me."

Utterly exhausted, Li Zhenzi closed her eyes, as though she'd completed an appointed mission.

Team Leader Ji, having listened to her story without saying a word, remained silent, feeling no desire to ask any of the questions that came to mind.

Suddenly, without opening her eyes, Li Zhenzi said, "The

110

drugs are hidden in the cistern of the toilet behind the little dining hall. My cousin smuggled them in in the sleeve of her jacket when she came to visit me. I'm feeling better, so you can take me to solitary confinement now."

Her words moved Team Leader Ji to tears. She was such an emotional woman that the slightest thing brought tears to her eyes. But it wouldn't be seemly for a guard to cry in front of one of her prisoners. Her prestige would suffer. She coughed a time or two to stop the tears from flowing, calmed her emotions as best she could, and gave the standard speech of encouragement: "Don't give up. No matter how bad things get, you must live out your life as best you can."

"Live out my life?" Li Zhenzi said with a sneer. "Isn't that what I'm doing?"

Team Leader Ji stood up and walked over to the window, where she stood for a moment before turning and saying earnestly, "Li Zhenzi, don't give up on yourself. I'm willing to be like a sister to you. I liked you from the first day I saw you. You're cultured and well-bred, you know when to keep your mouth shut, and you're not a schemer." She paused, then continued in a voice filled with emotion, "You're a decent woman."

Li Zhenzi froze as tears welled up in her eyes and spilled out onto her cheeks. After all those years of carrying the cross of indecency, after suffering through all those dark nights, someone had actually said she was decent. She opened her eyes and looked at Team Leader Ji uncomprehendingly. "I'm a decent woman?"

"That's right, a decent woman. Your love for your husband never wavered. Even when you were lying beneath another man, only Shi Li had a place in your heart. But you were wrong to trade your body for the well-being of your husband. That was as foolish as selling a gold watch to buy a watch chain . . ."

Li Zhenzi breathed a long sigh of despair, stopping Team Leader Ji in midsentence. She closed her eyes again.

Group Leader Liu came back into the room, where she found Li Zhenzi lying lethargically, her eyes closed. She was

111

fit to be tied. "No one else is going to save you! You have to save yourself! You broke prison rules and caused us a lot of trouble!" She turned to Team Leader Ji. "Your team causes more trouble than any team in the brigade! One month in solitary confinement, and deduct a hundred work points!"

Li Zhenzi crawled out of bed, got dressed and brushed her hair, looking straight at Group Leader Liu like a condemned prisoner on her way to the execution ground. The look in her eyes said, Let's go, I'm ready.

"Just look how callous she is! If solitary confinement doesn't bother you, I promise you'll be there till it does!" Group Leader Liu was enraged by Li Zhenzi's disdainful attitude.

Team Leader Ji led her out of the sickroom by her sleeve. "Group Leader Liu," she said, "she started coming around a moment ago by telling me where the drugs are stashed. Since she's still weak, can't we let her stay in the medical clinic a couple of days?"

Group Leader Liu had a remarkable capacity to adapt to changes. "I know you're better at ideological work than I am, and you can rest assured I'm not jealous." Her directness made Team Leader Ji blush. She had no idea how to explain herself. "But don't forget, softhearted people have no place here. Prisoners are still prisoners, and they're here because they've committed crimes. If you're not tough on them, they'll shit all over you. Forget their tears and how pitiful they seem now. Because when they're killing somebody, or cheating somebody, or stealing something, they can be more ruthless than you'll ever know. I always say that human beings are thieves at heart. And that goes double for convicts, who have an evil streak in them. You probably think that all she needs to turn her life around is a couple more days in the medical clinic, right?"

Before Group Leader Liu could finish her monologue, Li Zhenzi emerged from the clinic, with a deadpan look on her face, and headed straight toward solitary confinement. Her two superiors watched in astonishment as she walked down the corridor.

5

COUSIN FINALLY GOT SOMETHING PUBLISHED. FIVE OF HER short stories appeared in a single issue of the largest literary magazine in the province. She immediately gave a copy to Old Liu, a highly respected critic, and said with conspicuous sincerity, "Even though the critics Li and Xu have already written critiques, something by you would carry a lot more weight!" She then went to see the promising young critic by the name of Li, to whom she said earnestly, "Old Liu is writing a critical article on these stories, but since you and I are of the same generation, and you know me better than anyone, not to mention my stories . . ." She attacked from both directions, urging both sides on, and before long, a dozen or so critical articles appeared in four or five provincial newspapers and magazines, big and small, like a constellation of stars surrounding a single moon. One thing led to another, and Cousin's literary works soon became the new "emperor's clothes": everyone was raving about them, whether they'd read them or not. Her home was as crowded as a marketplace, her circle of acquaintances was greatly expanded.

But no one could understand what was going on in her love life. She was unmoved by any of the celebrated suitors who favored her, showering her affections and passion instead on a coarse, heavy-set construction worker. She laughed at those of us who had grown culturally alienated and took the narrow view of life, so caught up in appearances that we lost all understanding of life's great pleasures. From then on I referred to her fiancé as "life's great pleasure."

Then one day, when we cousins were all together at a party, I finally got a chance to observe "life's great pleasure" firsthand. He was indeed a ferocious-looking man who made all the other spouses present appear pale and weak by comparison. He ate like a horse and slept like a log. In no time at all he finished off three loaves of Italian bread, nearly a pound of ham, and three bottles of beer. Then he lay down on the sofa to sleep. Instead of going over and cuddling up with him, Cousin maintained her poise and sat with a young graduate student recently assigned to the provincial publishing house from the foreign literature section of the Chinese Academy of Social Sciences and engaged in a discussion on structural realism and T. S. Eliot's *The Waste Land*. When my cousins' husbands and fiancés finished eating, they felt obliged to chat with my cousin and the others about literature and the arts, so as not to be accused of being uncultured. The room was suffused with the fiery rays of the afternoon sun, while "life's great pleasure" lay face up and spread all over the sofa, breathing heavily through his thick, parted lips. His thick, rotund body was jerking and twitching; his face was beaded with oily sweat. I imagined him having a horrible dream about mating with prehistoric beasts or something. The young graduate student intoned lustily:

> *Here is no water but only rock*
> *Rock and no water and the sandy road*
> *The road winding above among the mountains*
> *Which are mountains of rock without water*

My cousin took over from there:

> *If there were water we should stop and drink*
> *Amongst the rock one cannot stop or think*
> *Sweat is dry and feet are in the sand*
> *If there were only water amongst the rock*
> *Dead mountain mouth of carious teeth that cannot spit*

"Life's great pleasure" mumbled in his sleep, and his hand fell heavily "down there." Cousin noticed this and immediately stopped spewing lines from Eliot. By now her eyes were fixed on him. Everyone stopped speaking.

It didn't take long for people to start talking about how Cousin and the young graduate student had fallen for each other, and that "life's great pleasure" was no longer enough for her. Within three months Cousin and her young graduate student were a hot item, and the astonishment of her friends

and relatives soon turned to delight; they all urged her to
marry him. But he had just received notice that he was being
sent to America to study for a Ph.D., and she supported him
by agreeing that his career came first. Why, I don't know, but
my aunt took a great deal of interest in this romance, and
asked me to invite my cousin and her boyfriend to dinner one
Sunday. I did as she asked.

Cousin lived in a ten-square-meter earthquake shelter that
had escaped demolition. Except for meals, she spent hardly
any time in her parents' upstairs flat. Her mother invariably
insisted in joining in her conversations with friends, although
her comments seldom had any relevance to what they were
saying. But what bothered Cousin the most was the way her
mother read her mail and even kept it from her. Feeling that
her home wasn't safe anymore, she preferred to put up with
the stifling heat and numbing cold in her austere earthquake
shelter.

I shouted out that it was me as I knocked at the door. I
could hear the sound of paper being crumpled inside. A
moment later, Cousin, dressed in an undershirt and shorts,
with a sweatband around her head, opened the door to let me
in, then hung a "Not In" sign on the door, and quickly shut it.
She walked over to the desk, picked up the crumpled balls of
paper, and tossed them into the wastebasket.

"What are you being so secretive about?" I teased her.

"It, it's nothing," she stammered. I looked at her scrawny,
flat chest and her bony shoulders and arms, and was reminded
of a gangly child. Not a hint of maturity. It wasn't so much
that her femininity had wasted away as it was she'd never had
any to begin with. When she saw how I was staring at her, a
nervous, almost tormented look came into her eyes. "What
are you doing here?"

"My aunt asked me to invite you and your boyfriend to
dinner this Sunday. Sunday night's the only time Uncle is
free."

"Your aunt must have given a lot of thought to this! She
thinks she'll benefit by having me and my boyfriend appear
together in front of your uncle. Ai, why does she have to be so
wary of me? She has this notion that I've got the power to

115

ruin her family." She shook her head sadly and continued, "The only reason I wanted to meet your uncle was to leave a good impression, get him to like me. That way, if I felt like changing jobs, I could ask him to put in a good word for me. The Chinese have such dirty minds that they turn normal relations between the sexes into something sordid. Even if two people are blameless, other people will have them doing all kinds of things in their imagination. Belinski once said . . ."

"Enough already! You don't have to bring old man 'ski' into something as insignificant as this. Tell me what you want to do and I'll do it." She was getting more and more agitated, and I thought a little joke might get her mind off it.

She glanced at her watch, then looked at me nervously. Suddenly her eyes flashed and she blurted out, "Will you write a letter for me?" The words were no sooner out of her mouth than her resolve seemed to vanish.

Assuming a crafty, almost seductive tone, I said, "Okay, I'll write your letter for you. Tell me what you want me to write." I sat down at the desk, laid out a sheet of stationery, picked up a pen, and struck a writing pose.

Cousin stood up and began pacing the floor, then sat down and gave me a penetrating look with steely eyes, as though she were about to let me in on a deep, dark secret. "Ji Li," she said in a soft voice, "no one else knows what I'm about to tell you, and you must promise you'll never tell a soul, even if we turn into bitter enemies someday." There was a dark quality to her voice, as though it were coming out of an ash urn in the middle of the night. A coldness gripped my heart, and I unconsciously lowered my head to avoid her eyes.

She put her hand on my shoulder, sending a shiver all the way down to my heart. "This anonymous letter must be written before nine tonight, and my handwriting is too easy to spot." She opened a drawer and took out the draft of a letter, which she laid on the desk in front of me. "Copy this out," she said as though she were talking to a child. "It wouldn't occur to anyone to check your handwriting."

Still not daring to raise my head and look at her, I took a quick glance at the letter. "Oh, an anonymous letter about him!" I blurted out with astonishment.

116

There was a long pause before she said in a low, raspy voice, "Loving someone is just too painful. I'm exhausted! I'm convinced that trying to love someone is a consignment to hell."

Sensing that something important was in the air, I asked urgently, "What in the world's going on?"

"Not a thing. At two o'clock tomorrow afternoon the publishing house is going to decide whether or not he should be allowed to study abroad. So this letter has to reach the publishing house by tomorrow morning, and the last pickup tonight is at nine o'clock." She anxiously glanced at her watch.

"Why do you want to stand in his way like this?"

"What do you know! He's four years younger than I, and if he spends two years in the States . . . besides, we've already, um . . ." Her face darkened, and it was obviously too painful for her to go on. I suddenly realized the incredible amount of torment that had forced her into such demeaning conduct. She seemed so pitiful, so tragic, that I wanted to console her, but I just couldn't bring myself to say anything to someone who could stoop so low.

"I love him so much I'm afraid to lose him. This whole thing is driving me crazy!" It was the first time she'd opened up like that in front of me.

"It's not so much that you love him, but that you need his love." I don't know where I got the courage, but I raised my head and looked at her intently as I went on, "If you do this, you'll not only ruin his future, but any peace you might enjoy for the rest of your life as well. Even if he never found out what you did, and stayed here to marry you, would that put your heart at ease? The sun would rise in the west before you got any true happiness out of sharing your life with a man you had to trap to get into your bed."

She shook her head in frustration. "You're so juvenile!"

We heard footsteps outside the door, and she quickly gathered up the pen and paper, slipped into a pair of jeans, and became a different person altogether. She opened the door with a broad smile on her face. The young graduate student stood there holding a huge watermelon in his hands.

He stepped inside with the calm assurance of someone walking into his own home. He was surprised to see me there, and after an awkward pause, he greeted me before my cousin had a chance to say anything, "Oh, I see your cousin's here." I immediately felt sorry for him, like I would a lamb being led to the slaughter that looks at you with calm, smiling eyes. It was astonishing to see my cousin standing there as if nothing had happened. But she was staring at him like a hungry cat that's spotted a fish. She hung on his every word, a sweet smile on her face, even if what he said wasn't funny. Women, how quickly they change! Maybe she really was madly in love with him. The only thing I knew for sure was that at that moment nothing in the world mattered to them except each other. As I stood up to leave, they insisted that I stay and have some watermelon.

"I hear you've gone to work in a prison. Gotten used to it yet?" he said to make conversation as he sliced the watermelon.

"It's like any other place." All I wanted to do was get out of there as quickly as possible. My noncommittal answer showed it.

"You're right. People on the outside, like us, probably suffer more than those inside." Cousin was saying this for my benefit, but I let it pass.

"What, you mean you're unhappy today?" He stopped slicing the watermelon and looked at her questioningly.

"It's nothing," she quickly countered, "really nothing. Just letting off some emotions." She smiled, and so did he. So did I.

After he'd cut the watermelon into a dozen or more wedges, the juice covered the table like a puddle of blood. I forced myself to eat a couple of the wedges, then thanked them and rose to leave. They stood in the doorway and watched me as I walked off, pushing my bicycle ahead of me. After I'd gone a ways, I turned and looked back. His blue jacket had grown indistinct in the fading dusk, but her white shirt floated stubbornly in the engulfing darkness. I walked a bit farther, and finally even the white shirt was swallowed up in the darkness. I felt terrible.

6

JIANG HONG WAS BACK IN PRISON. EVERYTHING WAS AS familiar to her as her parents' home: the dining hall, the workshop, the washroom, reveille, classtime, everything. She could read the guards like a book. Only her cell was different. "Lucky for me," she said, " that I'm only separated from the brilliant leadership of Group Leader Liu by a single wall." Being back in prison didn't particularly disturb her, for even though she could eat and drink whatever she felt like on the outside, and come and go as she pleased, she was in a constant state of anxiety, particularly when walking around with several stolen wallets on her.

Not much had changed in the prison in over a year—the same old trees, the same old walkways. As for the guards, only Team Leader Ji was new. The place was familiar and comfortable.

After being incarcerated in the afternoon, she was given a bath, a haircut, and a clean, dark blue prison uniform. Team Leader Ji gave her the indoctrination lecture, which was a waste of time since she knew the rules better than anybody. That night she bedded down between Chen Dehao on the right and Xu Zifang on the left. When she took off her prison uniform, she was wearing only an undershirt with two bright red straps hanging loosely over her soft white shoulders, dazzling and quite remarkable. Her rounded breasts, which jiggled slightly with each breath she took, were taut and soft at the same time; they inspired envy and jealousy in women and nearly uncontrollable passion in men. She was trimming her bangs with a pair of scissors using a little round mirror; she said her hairdo was all the rage these days.

"A rotten piece of goods," Xu Zifang muttered cryptically from the bed on her right.

Ignoring the comment, Jiang Hong lay down facing Chen Dehao and squinted at her with her limpid eyes. "I feel like I've been on a business trip out of town, and now we're back together."

"Since there aren't any men around, you turn to women for your pleasure." Xu Zifang, who was going through menopause, was always in a foul mood, and enjoyed stirring up trouble among the other women. She knew that Chen Dehao was disgusted with her, preferring the pretty young prisoners.

At first Jiang Hong didn't let it bother her and held her tongue, but then, to get Xu Zifang's goat, she said, "Dehao, cover up or you'll catch a draft," and stretched out her large feet to slide Chen Dehao's sheet up over her abdomen.

"Just listening to you makes sour water run out of my ears," Xu Zifang snapped angrily when she saw what Jiang Hong was doing.

"Really? Then you ought to cut down on your vinegar intake!" Jiang Hong replied matter-of-factly.

"A real smart mouth, aren't we!" Xu Zifang shot back.

"If you sewed my mouth shut, it'd still be smarter than three or four of yours," Jiang Hong took up the challenge.

Realizing she was no match for Jiang Hong, Xu Zifang ended the contest by holding her tongue. She'd find a way to get even later.

Chen Dehao, on the other hand, was delighted. She stretched her leg out under the sheet and tickled Jiang Hong's waist. Jiang Hong winked at her a couple of times, turned her face away, and gyrated sensuously on her back, which aroused Chen so that she reached out to touch the taut, curvaceous body. But while her hand was still in the air, a penetrating gaze settled on her trembling Adam's apple like the talons of a hawk, and she timidly drew her hand back and rolled over to avoid the sight of both the curvaceous body and the penetrating gaze. She hated that old devil's gaze that had settled on her Adam's apple, and hated even more the rumors Xu Zifang spread among the other prisoners about how manly she was. No longer in the mood to play games with Jiang Hong, she pulled the sheet up over her head and went to sleep.

The bell rang and the lights went out, throwing the cellblock into total darkness. "I can even bring women under my spell," Jiang Hong mused contentedly. Confident that Chen Dehao would bring her comfort, she waited impatiently for a while; but the sounds of Chen Dehao snoring took the wind out of her sails and gave her a lost, uncomfortable feeling, like a scrap of paper floating down into the unknown depths of a dried-up well.

The next morning, before getting out of bed, she took her small mirror out from under her pillow and examined her skin carefully to assure herself that the face cream she'd put on the night before had done its job. That finlike wrinkle, it was still there despite a night of silent treatment! A wave of anxiety swept across her heart. Why are there bags under my eyes? There was panic in her face. She hurriedly put her pillow under her neck so that her head touched the bedframe, hoping that the fluid would drain back into her eye sockets. Then during breakfast, instead of rice soup, which she'd have to bend over to eat, she took only a dry bun and ate it with her head raised.

That morning Team One was assigned to load trucks, placing wooden cases of soap bars onto a truck to be taken into town and sold. It was heavy work. Since Jiang Hong hadn't slept all night and had worked hard the day before, she was at it no more than an hour when she began to feel light-headed. The heavy cases resting painfully on her shoulders made her grimace in pain, deepening the wrinkle on her face and raising furrows on her brow. She glanced in the mirror from time to time when no one was looking. She'd already gone to the bathroom twice, had stopped to tie her shoes and change clothes, all tricks designed to let her catch her breath. She'd tried everything. She looked worried as Chen Dehao walked past with a case on each shoulder and glanced at her sympathetically. This gave Jiang Hong an idea.

She went over and dragged a rickety handcart out from behind the door, so she could work together with Chen Dehao. "Dehao, it'll be easier to use this handcart, which'll take five cases at a time." Her voice was loud enough, but weak.

Chen Dehao jumped at the offer.

Jiang Hong was feeling more relaxed now, since Chen Dehao did the loading and unloading, while she only had to help push the handcart back and forth. But Xu Zifang wasn't about to let anyone else have an easier time than she, especially the pretty and flighty Jiang Hong, whom she'd never let take even the slightest advantage of her.

"We all want to use handcarts," she reported to Team Leader Ji in a roundabout way of accomplishing her objective.

"We only have one. Get back to work!" Xu Zifang's pettiness irritated Team Leader Ji, who was sitting on one of the cases reading a book, which was why she'd answered her so roughly.

"She'll never change her indecent ways. She's just using Chen Dehao," Xu Zifang grumbled as she picked up a case and walked off.

Only then did Team Leader Ji realize that Xu Zifang was raising a larger issue. She looked over at Chen Dehao, whose face was bathed in sweat as she loaded the cases from the handcart onto the bed of the truck, with the smiling Jiang Hong standing beside her without lifting a finger.

"Jiang Hong!"

"Yo."

"Get back to carrying cases. Let Li Zhenzi help Chen Dehao with the handcart."

"Yes, ma'am——" She drew the sound out, glaring hatefully at Xu Zifang as she walked away from the handcart.

"I can carry the cases, Team Leader Ji," Li Zhenzi said stubbornly, her head lowered.

Jiang Hong winked at Chen Dehao, who understood her meaning. She put down the handcart and said, "We'll all carry them," then walked empty-handed into the workshop and picked up three cases at once.

"Chen Dehao, two at a time is plenty."

"Yes, ma'am." She squatted down with difficulty to remove the uppermost case from her shoulder, but she couldn't do it.

"It's okay this time, but no more than two at a time from now on." Seeing how mechanically Chen carried out her orders brought a smile to Team Leader Ji's lips.

Jiang Hong picked up a case of soap and staggered over to the truck, her face bright red. On the way she brushed up against Xu Zifang as she headed back to the workshop for another load. Jiang Hong, who was tired and in a bad mood to begin with, was ready to explode. Without a second thought, she spat out a gob of sticky phlegm that landed right next to Xu Zifang's shoe.

"No shitting or pissing on the floor," Xu Zifang cursed like a spiteful old street monger.

"You old fox fairy!" Jiang Hong cursed softly.

"If you can't get into a man's pants, a fake woman's okay for you!" Xu Zifang mumbled.

"Who're you calling a fake woman? Where do you get off calling Chen Dehao a fake woman?" Jiang Hong complained loudly for Chen Dehao's benefit.

It worked. Chen Dehao put down the cases she was carrying, her eyes nearly popping out of their sockets, walked up to Xu Zifang, and—smack! a slap landed on her face.

"She hit me!" Xu Zifang screamed. "She's trying to kill me!" As she was about to fall down, she spotted an oil slick at her feet, so she twisted her body enough to land on a clean spot. Her eyes were ghostly white, she was foaming at the mouth, and her body began to twitch.

Team Leader Ji threw down her book and ran over to the truck, telling Li Zhenzi to check Xu Zifang's pulse and sending Jiang Hong for the doctor.

"She's faking it, the gutless wonder. That's all she knows how to do!" Jiang Hong didn't move.

"Jiang Hong, go get the doctor!" Team Leader Ji repeated emphatically.

Jiang Hong turned and walked off.

Team Leader Ji knelt down beside Xu Zifang and held her hand. "Take it easy," she said anxiously. "Everything will be all right." Hearing Team Leader Ji's voice next to her, Xu Zifang began twitching more violently, foaming more heavily, and gnashing her teeth more loudly. Team Leader Ji gripped her hand, which was turned inward like a claw, to make it easier for Li Zhenzi to take her pulse.

"She's fine," Li Zhenzi said without looking up.

"Here comes Group Leader Liu. Now let's see you put on your act." Instead of going to the medical clinic, Jiang Hong had gone straight for Group Leader Liu. Although this displeased Team Leader Ji, what could she say?

"Let her twitch!" Group Leader Liu said to the people who were gathered around Xu Zifang. "Chen Dehao!" she shouted.

"Yo." Chen's voice was quaking. She stood in front of Group Leader Liu with her arms at her sides, her head lowered.

"By hitting her like that, you broke prison regulation number fourteen. Are you aware of that?"

"Yes."

"A week in solitary confinement and a deduction of thirty merit points. Any problem with that?" A week in solitary confinement and the deduction of thirty merit points meant a one-month extension of her sentence. Once the newspapers and broadcast media had begun promoting reforms, the prison Discipline Section had started working overtime to come up with brand-new and untested management policies. Deducting merit points was the newest of such experimental policies. Performing the jobs they were assigned every day and studying their responsibilities without getting into trouble earned prisoners one point, with extra points for extraordinary performance. But fighting, spreading rumors, goldbricking, and refusing to accept remolding resulted in the loss of points, the quantity to be determined by the gravity of the offense. A year of one's sentence was determined not by the actual days spent inside, but by the accumulation of 365 merit points.

"Jiang Hong," Group Leader Liu called out, looking all around.

Never suspecting that Group Leader Liu might punish her, Jiang Hong reported what had happened, spicing up her report with plenty of compliments to Group Leader Liu. More significant, as far as she was concerned, was that when she had entered prison the last time, she'd helped Group Leader Liu knit some wool sweaters that everyone had raved about. That made the other prisoners envious, even downright jealous, of how she'd wormed her way into Group Leader Liu's good graces. Naturally there was plenty of talk among the guards as well.

"Jiang Hong!" Group Leader Liu raised the decibel level

considerably. "Did you really think I'd protect you just because you volunteered to tell me what happened, or because of all your compliments, or because you helped me knit some sweaters, or because you gave me some stuff for my kids while you were on the outside? Not on your life, and I want everybody to know that! This is your fault, and since you've delayed the loading, I'm ordering you to stay here while the others are resting and keep loading!" She looked at her watch. "Everybody else can knock off now."

Knowing she'd better move right away, Jiang Hong ran over and picked up a case as the other women drifted away.

"Xu Zifang!" Group Leader Liu said as she nudged the woman's rear with the toe of her shoe. "If you don't get up right this minute, I'm going to deduct a hundred merit points!"

The startled Xu Zifang bolted up into a sitting position and stopped crying and raising a fuss.

"Go load cases. And if I hear another word out of you, I'll cut your tongue out!" She looked smugly over at Team Leader Ji, thrust her hands into her pants pockets and stuck them out as far as they would go, then paraded her flat rear around Team Leader Ji a couple of times. She stopped and said, without mincing words, "Come get me if they give you any more trouble. Heh-heh, you're not jealous of the prestige I carry around here, are you?"

"Of course not. Whatever you do, it's all part of your job, isn't it?" Team Leader Ji didn't know how to respond to Group Leader Liu's veiled comment. So she just denied the implication.

"I wonder." Group Leader Liu walked off after a final "heh-heh."

Team Leader Ji was not at all happy, but she couldn't show it. If she did, they'd think she was petty or jealous. Besides, there'd been nothing wrong in Jiang Hong's report, and nothing wrong in Group Leader Liu's leaving once she'd taken care of the situation. And, of course, Group Leader Liu's straightforward question had been right on the mark, hadn't it? So why had she denied it? The way Group Leader Liu avoided mincing words, was that just her nature, or was she being brutally candid? Team Leader Ji paced the floor deep in thought. When Jiang Hong and Xu Zifang, who were conscientiously loading cases, spotted her walking up to them, they pretended not to see her, although she could feel their eyes on her. Nothing would ever get straightened out with Team One if Group Leader Liu didn't show up. Team Leader Ji had already gotten used to using her as a crutch, and she knew that the only way she'd ever gain any authority among her prisoners was to undermine Group Leader Liu's authority.

It was lunchtime, and the prisoners from all the groups had to pass by where Team Leader Ji was standing to line up at the dining hall. Jiang Hong walked back and forth loading cases without daring to look up. She was tempted to tell them to knock off and line up for lunch in order to show that she was more considerate than Group Leader Liu. After all, the truck driver would take a nap after lunch, so there'd still be plenty of time to load the truck. But she didn't succumb to the temptation. Trying to please or win over the prisoners was not the way to establish her authority. It was time for a change in tactics. So instead of going to lunch herself, she'd pitch in and help them load the truck, which would make them feel guilty and grateful for her sacrifice.

Like Jiang Hong and Xu Zifang, she carried only a single case at a time, but she quickened her pace until she was making two trips for every one of theirs. Jiang Hong and Xu Zifang didn't take notice at first, but before long they were moving as quickly as Team Leader Ji.

When the rest of the prisoners came back to work at two o'clock, they spotted Team Leader Ji stripped down to her blouse, which was soaked with sweat, her face bright red from the exhausting work of carrying the cases. At first they were too startled to speak, but then they started talking among themselves and casting reproachful looks at Jiang Hong and Xu Zifang.

"It's not their fault alone. If any member of my team gets into a fight, as team leader I deserve to pay the consequences. We need to make allowances for each other." She mopped her brow and headed back to work.

But the women went up and stopped her.

"Team Leader Ji, I started it," Xu Zifang blurted out. "I caused the trouble, and I deserve to be punished. I'll get down on my knees if you pick up another case." She grabbed Team Leader Ji's hand and started to kneel down. Meanwhile Jiang Hong stood off to the side with her head bowed, not saying a word. Feeling that she'd already begun reaping rewards, Team Leader Ji decided it was time to bring matters to a close. She put on her jacket and said, "Those two worked hard while the rest of you were eating lunch, and made up for the lost time. I think we should let them go wash up, get something to eat, and take the rest of the afternoon off. What do you say?"

Naturally everyone agreed, which moved Xu Zifang. But Jiang Hong just stood there with her head bowed, not saying a word.

Jiang Hong's punishment, instead of putting her in a bad mood, actually seemed to enliven her. She continued to lie in bed as long as possible every morning to look at herself in the mirror, she continued to wear her red undershirt, and she continued with her flirtatious looks, especially on the first of each month, when her longtime lover, who vowed to love her until the seas dried up and the mountains turned to dust, came to visit. He'd bring her food, little things she could use, and plenty of smiles. As each visit approached, she'd wash the dark blue prison jacket she wore on special occasions, then iron it and keep it under her pillow so it wouldn't get wrinkled. Whether it was a hot day or a cold one, she was determined to wear her pale green cotton blouse with its "Made in the U.S.A." label, which gave her a youthful look, at least in the V-shaped area beneath her chin.

The long-awaited day arrived, but this time her boyfriend didn't show up. According to one of her other visitors, he'd found a new girlfriend. Jiang Hong brushed this news off with a shrug, but deep down she was crushed. Over the next few visiting days—the first Sunday of each month—she waited impatiently, and finally sent him a couple of letters, asking him to visit her one last time. When Sunday morning finally rolled around, she woke up feeling utterly depressed, like someone on her way to the guillotine. She went into the bathroom right after breakfast, and still hadn't come out half an hour later. Her cellmates knew she was in there plucking her eyebrows and putting on lipstick, but they didn't disturb her so as to avoid any unnecessary gossip. All except Xu Zifang, who refused to go along with the others. She strode ostentatiously into the bathroom.

When Jiang Hong, who was plucking her eyebrows with the aid of her round hand mirror, saw Xu Zifang enter, obviously to make a scene, she quickly took the offensive: "What do you think, are my eyebrows thin enough? Curved just right?" Then, with a hard look in her eyes, she snarled, "Go report me if you want. But be careful I don't skin you alive!"

"The person who could skin me alive hasn't been born. Come on, I'm taking you to see Team Leader Ji." Xu Zifang grabbed the lipstick out of Jiang Hong's hand and started out of the bathroom.

Jiang Hong reached out, grabbed her by the collar, and flung her up against the wall, where she smeared her face with lipstick, then tossed the lipstick and hand mirror into the toilet and flushed it. She ran out of the bathroom shouting, "Hey everybody, come look at the witch. What's that she's got all over her face?"

The women came out of their cells and crowded around the toilet to see what was going on. Xu Zifang was inside trying to scrub the red markings off her face. "She spat blood all over me," she complained, "she spat blood all over me!"

A dozen or so of the prisoners nearly fell all over each other as they rushed out to report what had happened. At the first sign of trouble, no matter how badly their assistance was needed, invariably their first reaction was to report it. It was a long-standing prison tradition. "Here comes Team Leader Ji!" they buzzed, quickly retreating to the doorway of their cells.

Team Leader Ji ran up the stairs and straight to the bathroom. Tears began streaming down Xu Zifang's face before she even opened her mouth, as though a lifetime of grievances were spilling out. Team Leader Ji consoled her briefly, then went looking for Jiang Hong, who was standing in front of her cell, looking off in the other direction.

"Go take a look and tell me if her face used to be that red," Team Leader Ji said to the others.

"Everybody likes to be pretty," Jiang Hong said with a sneer.

"There's what you call bad habits," Team Leader Ji said in a feisty tone. "That's what immorality does to you!"

Shamed into anger, Jiang Hong reacted like a wounded tigress, flinging Team Leader Ji's hand away and bursting into tears, then burying her face against the wall. "You can punish me for my crimes, but what gives you the right to insult me? I'd rather be dead . . ." She drew her head back like she was going to smash it against the wall, but was stopped by Chen Dehao and a couple of the other prisoners. But the more tightly they held her, the harder she struggled. They were soon a mass of flying feet and swinging arms.

The color had drained from Team Leader Ji's face. It was time to make an example of Jiang Hong, for if she couldn't control her today, tomorrow she'd lose control over Li Hong, and Wang Hong, and . . . "Let her smash her head against the wall if she wants to," she ordered the women restraining Jiang Hong.

"Let me go! Let me kill myself . . . I want to kill myself . . ." The harder Jiang Hong struggled, the more reluctant the women were to release their grip.

"Let her go!" Never in her life had Team Leader Ji spoken so forcefully. Momentarily stunned, they released their grip.

"Okay, Jiang Hong, we're waiting! Do it!" Team Leader Ji's voice was controlled yet urgent. The others looked at Jiang Hong, their hearts in their mouths, not daring to make a sound. Jiang Hong was scared silly. She stood there frozen to the spot for a moment before falling against the wall and crying like a baby. Team Leader Ji, now looking cool and collected, said in a relaxed tone, "Jiang Hong, write a report of what happened and bring it to my office at noon." She turned and swaggered off.

The whispers began immediately: "Jiang Hong was put in her place by Team Leader Ji." But Team Leader Ji was distressed to realize that she'd turned into a rough, unyielding woman.

7

MY AUNT WAS HOSPITALIZED FOR A WEEK WITH myocarditis, and Uncle only visited her briefly once. After the attending physician reported on her case, he asked Uncle if he had any recommendations for treatment. But Uncle's secretary had already received several urgent phone calls: an emergency meeting of the Municipal Standing Committee; a report on his inspection tour of the sixteen factories; the establishment of a sister-city relationship with Yokohama; a series of public lectures at various universities by a delegation of Sino-Vietnamese war heroes; a summer camp for more than two hundred teachers and students from the Beijing Youth Palace . . . Uncle was responsible for presiding over opening ceremonies, meeting with all sorts of people, and participating in official visits, ribbon cuttings, banquets, document signings, and photo sessions. He sat by Auntie's sickbed for ten minutes or so, checked her pulse once, and looked over her planned diet. "You're better off in the hospital than at home," he said, "so I want you to stay here a few more days." When he walked out of the room, he was immediately surrounded by his secretary, several underlings, and his chauffeur. Auntie was left alone in her hospital room.

"Isn't it funny how everything seems to be taking place this week?" she mumbled to herself at noon.

"That's the price one pays for being an official," I said as I peeled an apple for her.

She laughed. "The price one pays for being an official? The perks of being an official is more like it."

I sliced the apple, stuck in some toothpicks, and put the plate in front of her.

"Ji Li, I'd rather eat the canned pineapple your uncle brought. You eat the apple." I recalled with sadness how

Uncle's secretary had bought the canned pineapple at a nearby shop and put it into Uncle's bag in order to ingratiate himself with his boss. But I opened the can without saying anything.

"Your uncle's so thoughtful. He knows how much I like pineapple." She may have been unhappy deep down, but she managed a fleeting smile. "He's just too busy, too busy," she mumbled.

"My chest is bothering me," she said as she rubbed it.

"Should I call the doctor, Auntie?"

"No, I'll be fine in a moment. Sit here beside me. Do you have to go to work this afternoon?"

"No, I took a couple of days off," I lied. Now I had to find a way to call the office and ask for the time off.

"What's your mother up to these days?"

"She's spending a week in the lab. She says as soon as this experiment is finished, she'll come and stay with you in the hospital for a couple of days." My parents and Auntie had been schoolmates, and she was their matchmaker.

"How about your father?"

"He's revising three of his students' M.A. theses. He's so busy he doesn't know which end is up. He had a Political Consultative Conference meeting yesterday, but he took the wrong bus."

"What about your younger brother?"

"Working on his graduation project. His girlfriend moved in with him."

"Ai . . . even an honest boy like him has changed. "And your father's sister?"

"She's always complaining to my uncle how useless he is. They were talking about getting a divorce the other day."

"How can two people in their sixties act like schoolkids! How about their daughter? Now that her young graduate student has gone abroad, does he write to her? Have you seen her recently?" Her questions seemed innocent enough, but I knew she was wondering if my cousin had been over to her home over the past few days.

"He doesn't write very often," I said coyly. "Maybe something's wrong between them. But she's been in a great mood lately. She's been helping Uncle draft a report on his inspection tour."

"Oh . . ." Pretending to be disinterested, she closed her eyes, as though all this talk had made her sleepy. "She's part of a team of five," I said comfortingly. But she ignored me, as though she were falling asleep. The can of pineapple on the headboard hadn't been touched.

I walked out of the room and went downstairs to call my office, then rushed over to the gift shop to buy a few things for Auntie before heading back upstairs. I was surprised to see her out of bed, stuffing her things into a large bag.

She smiled when she spotted the puzzled look on my face. "This place is too depressing, so I'm going to check out. Go tell the nurse to prepare my bill and give me a prescription to take home with me. Then call the car pool and have them send a car for me. Oh, and don't say anything to your uncle. There's no need to bother him."

"Did . . . didn't you say you were having chest pains just a minute ago?"

"They'll just get worse in here."

I had no choice but to do as she asked. After taking care of the paperwork, with the doctors and nurses standing around looking puzzled, I helped my frail aunt into the car and up to her room when we got her home. I told her to rest in her easy chair while I made up the bed. But I hadn't even laid out the comforter before she shuffled unsteadily up to the bed, pushed me aside, turned on the bed lamp, and carefully picked up the pillow, scrutinizing every inch of the bed sheet.

"Looking for bedbugs, Auntie?"

"Um . . ." She paused for a moment, then mumbled, "Maybe."

She finished her examination of the bedding without finding anything, then climbed wearily into bed, gasping for breath after all that strenuous activity. I placed a piece of foam rubber against the headboard for her to lean against, fed her a few spoonfuls of honey, and told her to get some sleep. But she seemed impatient to do so many things that even though her eyes were closed, I could see the rapid movement of her eyeballs under the lids.

"Get some sleep, Auntie. I'll have the cook make you something to eat." I helped her change into a nightgown, then rushed downstairs to the kitchen to tell the cook what to do. But on my way downstairs, I remembered how much she enjoyed sweet porridge, so I turned and went back upstairs to get the can of pineapple. I walked in without knocking.

She was standing barefoot in front of the mirror. She turned and looked at me with some embarrassment, but once she'd composed herself, she asked, "What is it?" That could have been taken as "What is it you want?" or "What is it she's making for me?"

"Sweet porridge," I answered, "so I came back for the pineapple." I walked up to the dresser to get the can.

Auntie had been picking hairs out of her comb by the light of the window. She turned her attention back to the comb, examining each tooth from one end to the other. She suddenly stopped and frowned as she plucked out two particularly long strands. Her hands were trembling slightly, causing the strands of hair to dance in the air. Then she tried to pluck out another long strand, but it snapped in two. "Longer than mine," she mumbled in a monotone as a troubled look spread across her face. After a moment she seemed to have second thoughts; she wrapped the strands of hair in a piece of paper and held it in her hand as though it were a priceless treasure, then climbed back into bed. She lay down and looked up at me absentmindedly.

What could I say to make her feel better? "Auntie, I'll take the pineapple downstairs and have the cook make you some sweet porridge, all right?"

She was looking at me, but I could have sworn she didn't see me. After a moment she smiled, as though she'd decided what to do. "Fine, that'll be fine."

Uncle was home. Before he'd even come upstairs, his hearty laughter came rolling into the room. "Well, I'll be! What's so important about coming home? Why not spend a few more days in the hospital?" He strode into the room, patted me on the head tenderly, and sat down on the bed next to Auntie. "But this is fine, too. It's more peaceful at home. I'll have the doctor drop by every day." He pointed to his cup on the headboard next to him and said, "I'd like a cup of tea, Li."

I knew that Uncle doted on me by the way he asked me to do little things for him. It made him feel good. I poured him some tea.

"Has your cousin been over? She's editing a couple of tapes for me, and she said she'd bring them over at two this afternoon," he said as he looked at his watch.

I instinctively glanced over at Auntie nervously and quickly told him I didn't know if she'd been by or not.

Auntie closed her eyes and gently stroked his large hand. Before long two glistening tears puddled up in the corners of her eyes and rolled down her ashen cheeks.

"Why worry about a little illness like this? All you need is rest and some vitamin C," Uncle comforted her in his booming voice, although to me it sounded like a man taking care of official business.

Auntie opened her eyes and looked at him lovingly. "Go downstairs," she said to me, "and have the cook prepare a couple of extra dishes. We'll have your cousin stay for dinner."

Her words saddened me. I never could understand the heart of a woman, so small yet so big, so shallow yet so complex. Such unfathomable little creatures women are!

8

TIME MOVED ON RELENTLESSLY AS AUTUMN TURNED TO winter. It cast out a handful of snowflakes to bury the tender branches and green leaves on the trees. The snowfall spread out its arms like a loving mother and floated gently down from the sky, kissing the dirty ground beneath and bestowing the affection of heaven on the world below; as it sent down its vast benevolent love, countless tender green lives were exhausted in the purity of its body.

The steamy breath of women appeared in the midst of the heavily falling snow in the prison yard, like so many trampled flower buds in a vast desert. There was an unwritten rule that the prisoners could wear scarves and woolen caps of whatever color and design they desired during a snowstorm. This rule, which seemed humanitarian without really being so, produced some excitement among the young prisoners for whom appearances were so important. As soon as winter arrived, they actually looked forward to snowstorms. Normally these women were dressed in dark blue from head to toe, inside and out. But now the tiny triangles of "free markets" where their shirts opened at the neck gave some of the rowdier girls a chance to show off, which caught the attention of the prison administrators. Ultimately these "free markets" were the cause of several incidents, and had to be closed down.

Even though the prisoners could wear colorful scarves and woolen caps, since it was snowing and it was a holiday—New Year's Eve—the mood among those in Team One was subdued. It was the last day of the year, and Jiang Hong was scheduled to take a technician's exam. But she was having menstrual cramps and couldn't get out of bed. Her face had been as white as a sheet when she went to bed the night before. She crumpled her blanket and pillow and kept them pressed up against her belly all night long. Neither moaning nor saying a word, she just lay there with her head resting on a pile of study materials.

Chen Dehao had no desire to take care of her, since she'd been notified the day before that she was being sent to the People's Municipal Hospital for a sex operation. Ever since Xu Zifang had discovered her infatuation with Jiang Hong, she had begun calling her the "fake woman," and all the other prisoners had become fascinated over the question of her gender. They noticed how she always bathed by herself and was the first to get undressed and the last to put on her clothes. Some said she had a flat chest and never wore a bra. And someone reported to Group Leader Liu something far more significant: Chen Dehao had never had a period, even though she was already twenty-one years old! Group Leader Liu reported this to her superiors at once, and they had the outside doctor take her to the gynecology department at the People's Municipal Hospital to be examined, where she was

135

diagnosed as being of indeterminate gender. Was she a man? A woman? That could only be determined by opening up her pelvis to see if she had ovaries or testicles. If it was found that she had both, or neither, surgery would be performed to make her either a man or a woman, based upon what society considered her to be, her own preferences, the degree of dominance of one sex over the other, and surgical considerations.

Chen Dehao nearly fainted when she heard the medical diagnosis. She had been born and reared in the mountains, and even though she knew something was wrong, she had never dreamed she could be a hermaphrodite. She returned to the prison crying like someone who had just lost both parents. The prison authorities gave her a cell to herself prior to the operation that would determine her sex. She ate and drank nothing, and woke up in the middle of the night, picked up her bedding, and ran crying back to the cell she'd been in up to that day. Although her cellmates felt sorry for her, they were also frightened, and there was so much going on that night that no one in the cellblock slept a wink. She woke up in the morning before the sun was up, crying and sniffling, "I'll never be able to face anyone again! I'll never be able to face anyone again!"

When Xu Zifang saw how unhappy Chen Dehao was, her conscience began to bother her. She'd been having a particularly difficult time with menopause recently, with a ringing in her ears, light-headedness, palpitations, and night sweats, so she was moody and easily irritated. Although she felt like crying, or screaming, or getting into a fight or an argument with someone, anyone, no one was buying what she had to sell, since New Year's was just around the corner, and all the prisoners were preparing for one kind of exam or another. And the more difficult it was to vent her feelings, the more depressed she grew, and the worse her sweats and palpitations became.

Li Zhenzi was completely indifferent to everything associated with Team One. During the day she worked alone without talking to anyone, and at night she lay quietly on her bed in the corner. She never struck up a conversation, and no one tried to talk to her. She kept to herself, whether she was strolling in the yard or working, and after the brigade leader or group leader or team leader had a talk with her, she just stood against the wall and looked out the window at the snowflakes dancing in the air, adding layer upon layer of coldness to her mood. Sometimes the corners of her eyes drooped, while the corners of her mouth wrinkled, making her look like she was about to cry, or laugh. The light green silk scarf that had hibernated for ten years dropped from her hand to the ground, but instead of picking it up, she just kept staring out the window.

Group Leader Liu rushed into her office wearing a cloak of snow. Team Two Leader Qian and Team Three Leader Zhao helped her dust off the snow. A look of satisfaction spread across Group Leader Liu's face before she even opened her mouth.

Team Leader Zhao's voice dripped with praise as she said, "You can accomplish more by yourself than the two of us put together. As long as you were at the meeting, our report was sure to be passed."

"You don't have to kiss your immediate superior's ass." Enormously pleased with herself, Group Leader Liu accepted the cup of tea offered to her by Team Leader Qian, took a sip, then said excitedly, "Between the first and the tenth, eleven prisoners in our group will get leave passes: Li Bing, Zhao Huayun, Jiang Juanfeng, Xu Zifang, Jiang Hong, Li Zhenzi; Chen Dehao's in the hospital . . ."

"Hold on, Xu Zifang still has ten years on her sentence, and she's been awfully moody lately. What if . . . ?" Team Leader Zhao looked over at Team Leader Ji, who was standing there without saying a word, and stopped in midsentence for fear of starting an argument.

"Yeah, how come so many prisoners in Team One get passes?" Team Leader Ji, who had been reading a novel she'd hidden in a drawer, looked up and grinned timidly at Group Leader Liu, but didn't say anything. She'd already guessed the answer to that question: it has to be because I've got a certain uncle. Someone to fall back on if anything goes wrong, while if everything turns out well, it will be a result of

137

Group Leader Liu's brilliant leadership.

"Here's what I think," Group Leader Liu said, breaking Team Leader Ji's train of thought. "If anything goes wrong, it'll come back to your team, but I'll be here in your corner, and naturally you'll have protection above. That way you're covered no matter what happens. Besides, everybody's promoting reforms these days. If nothing goes wrong, and the prisoners return on time, that will be quite an achievement, which will have a greater impact on your team than on the others." Group Leader Liu candidly confirmed what Team Leader Ji had suspected.

She was utterly disgusted with this cunning way of operating, but lacked the courage to say so. Now that it was an accomplished fact, she felt sadness and regret. She was furious with Group Leader Liu over her ingratiating ways, and even more furious with herself for being unable to put her feelings aside and oppose what was going on; that's where the regret came in. Her cousin had once invited a hairdresser who'd studied in the States and was home on a family visit to cut her hair in the short style made popular by Princess Diana. She neither liked the style nor thought it fit her, but she couldn't bring herself to seem ungrateful to her cousin's good intentions and the hairdresser's enthusiasm. But after they had left, she looked in the mirror and cried. That was when she had discovered the negative quality that made it impossible for her to say "no." So she resolved to force herself to get used to saying "no," like her cousin. But whenever she was faced with one of those situations, the word still wouldn't come out.

"Oh, right, there's something else very important you need to know. Not only will Li Zhenzi get a pass, but her husband has been given permission to come to the prison and spend New Year's with her. This news ought to wake up the press!" Group Leader Liu was so excited her face appeared to be steaming.

"Whose bright idea was that?" Team Leader Zhao was all smiles as she walked up to the desk where Team Leader Ji was sitting.

"Don't forget the rubbers," Team Leader Qian said derisively, forcing a serious look onto her face.

Whether the comment stemmed from prurient interest or uncalled-for seriousness, it sounded utterly profane to Team Leader Ji. She felt like saying so, but on second thought, that would only make matters worse. She turned and looked at the snow falling beyond the window. "Conjugal visits can be considered on an individual basis," she commented casually to Group Leader Liu, recalling an instructional book she'd read on foreign penal institutions. It never dawned on her that this could be one of the bright ideas associated with reforms in the penal system. But she didn't have time to think about things like that.

9

THE SNOW STOPPED FALLING SOMETIME DURING THE DAY. Team Leader Ji was gazing out the Jeep window. The sun's cold rays were reflected off the patches of snow on the ground. She looked over at Li Zhenzi's husband, Shi Li, who was also gazing out the window. He hadn't said a word since getting into the Jeep. His heart was as calm and steady as the hand of a surgeon. Was that a result of his medical training, or an indication that his heart had long since hardened?

"I have doubts about myself," he said with some hesitation.

"You must have faith. You love her."

Fearing that he might sink into despair, Team Leader Ji continued encouragingly, "You haven't given your love to anyone else after all these years. And since you still keep her photograph beside your bed, that proves you haven't forgotten her. You know how genuine her feelings for you are. She did it for you. She . . ."

"I realize that," Shi Li said calmly as he lit a cigarette. After smoking for a moment, he said softly, "I'd rather have died than let my wife sell her body like that."

"How can someone who doesn't even have the courage to forgive his wife's mistakes talk about dying?" Team Leader Ji was still gazing out the window at the sun following closely behind their Jeep.

"I hated myself for being so narrow-minded." He grew silent again.

When their Jeep pulled up to the guesthouse and stopped, Team Leader Ji said, "Here we are."

"Oh!" he said, as though waking from a dream. He got out of the Jeep.

A big red lantern with the word "Spring" on it was lying on its side in the snow beside the guesthouse door. Hadn't they had time to hang it next to the other one, with the word "Festival" on it? Or had it fallen to the ground? Shi Li was searching for an answer to this meaningless question as he walked into the guesthouse. He still hadn't allowed himself to think about anything else by the time he was standing in front of room 407. Reason and logic were paramount to him. When he knocked on the door, his heart was still as calm and steady as it had been on his way up the stairs.

The door opened to reveal Li Zhenzi with a look of panic in her eyes. For Shi Li it was a greeting that rang in his ears, and his heart began to pound.

She'd moved into their new apartment on the night before their wedding, and in the middle of the night, he had come over and opened the door. She sprang out of bed and stood there barefoot, her arms folded in front of her chest, looking like a tiny deer that had spotted a hunter. She looked at him with panic in her eyes.

"Let, let's become husband and wife a day early." No longer that cool, self-possessed surgeon she knew. His wildly beating heart increased his passion. He carried her over to the bed and kissed her fervently. She buried her head in his chest and began to tremble. When he transported her to that place covered with fragrant blossoms and the stink of fertilizer, she didn't know if she was in heaven or in hell. He heard the sound of her sobs and climbed off, shocked back to his senses. "I'm sorry," he said single-mindedly, "I'm so sorry . . ."

She smiled and threw herself into his arms.

Li Zhenzi wasn't the same person she'd been on the eve of their wedding, when she'd stood barefoot on the floor. Now she was wearing a pair of cloth flats, khaki pants, and a tan blouse over her prison jacket; he'd sent these new things to her a month earlier, except for the light green silk scarf around her neck, which he'd given her as a sort of engagement present. She'd kept it with her all these years, and although the silk was as worn as rotting grass and had lost its original luster, wearing it today gave her a look of simple elegance. There was panic in her eyes when she first saw him, but she quickly regained her composure and looked at him calmly, a gaze that was long and narrow, as if she were looking down a deep, remote valley.

He, too, had calmed down by then, and he looked around the fourteen-square-meter room that had the look of newness, with a new comforter on the bed, a brand-new washbasin, brand-new towels . . . a bright red, "double-happiness" cutout pasted on the wall behind the bed smiling down almost mockingly. He wondered how a little room that exuded sweetness like this could possibly accommodate two such anguished hearts. He walked over and opened the window, letting in a blast of cold winter air that immediately gave Li Zhenzi goose bumps. Maybe she'd been on her feet too long, or maybe she was just too nervous, but she staggered and barely managed to steady herself by holding on to the table.

"What's wrong?" He went over and held her up.

"I've been getting dizzy a lot lately . . ." Before she could finish, her face went pale and she slumped across the table.

He picked her up to carry her over to the bed, and when he had her in his arms, he exclaimed with astonishment, "She's so light!" She was like a sunbaked scarecrow. A powerful, heavy sadness gripped his heart. He opened his mouth and breathed deeply to keep the tears welling up in his eyes from spilling out. After laying her down on the bed and loosening her shirt, his hand brushed against the stiff, coarse prison jacket underneath, and he could hold his tears back no longer. "I, I've made you suffer so much . . ." He tucked her thin, tiny frame under the comforter, then held her tightly through the comforter with both arms.

Tears welled up in her eyes and ran down her cheeks, soaking the pillow cover. Without making a sound, she shook her head softly over and over; her eyes were barely open. All the time he was holding her, the silent tears never stopped.

The crackling of a string of exploding firecrackers outside

managed to lighten their moods a little. She glanced at the clock on the table and said, so softly it was more like a moan, "We're forty-four years old now, so long a time, so trying . . . go back home tomorrow and let the scab heal this time. Don't open the wound again. As long as we're together, the past will always be with us, and continuing to live in the shadow of our past will eventually destroy us both . . . it's late. Get some sleep, here beside me."

His heart had never felt heavier; all it contained were grief and pity. The passion of a moment ago was gone. He acknowledged her with a muffled grunt and turned out the light, throwing the room into darkness.

Outside winter had reasserted itself with falling snow. It was a ghostly apparition come to bemoan the state of the universe and bewail the fate of mankind. It moved through the misty night in that final moment of the old year.

The sound of exploding firecrackers off in the distance startled Li Zhenzi awake. She opened her eyes, but couldn't see anything in the surrounding darkness. There was a momentary silence, then more firecrackers, but much closer this time, as though they were exploding beneath the window. The noise roused her, made her tense. It was the first time in years she'd actually felt herself a part of New Year's activities, the first time she could hear the sounds of ushering out the old year and seeing in the new. All she could remember were dark events of the past, nothing relating to a hopeful and joyful sense of a new beginning. She sat up cautiously, holding her breath so as not to awaken her husband. What she wanted to do was go to the prison dining hall while he was still asleep to get the skins and fillings for some wontons, which she'd make to warm him for his trip. For this time she'd be seeing him off on a very long journey. He was getting old, too. Just before he'd turned off the light the night before, she'd noticed the gray around his temples, and the sight had saddened her. She was tempted to stroke his gray temples, but pulled her hand back before it touched him. She thought back to the night he'd been freed by the leader of the Dictatorship of the Proletariat team, and how she'd stroked his hair then. But he'd pushed her hand away in

142

alarm; she'd cried, and he'd ignored her all night.

"What, he's gone?" His comforter was cold. She sat on the bed, still in her nightgown, and clutched his comforter to her without moving a muscle. After a while she heard the sound of her teeth chattering, and her body felt like a cadaver, the blood frozen in its veins. She slowly crawled under his comforter, curling up into a ball and getting as close to the wall as possible, unconsciously leaving room for him. Her eyes were barely open, her heart felt like the excavation where the Peking man had been discovered, as though it were lying in a pool of greenish, filthy water. They'd gone to Zhongkoudian on their honeymoon, and the excavation scene had frightened her, had seemed somehow to be an unlucky omen.

"I was the one who urged him to leave. We simply can't keep living in the shadow of our past." Looking for ways to console herself, she repeated this over and over.

As dawn broke, the spotless red rays of morning sun filtered into the room through the window curtain and fell on the new comforters, the brand-new sheets . . . all those things that had held out such promise for happiness, but which now only depressed her more. Suddenly she thought back to her childhood, when nothing had frightened her so much as an electrical blackout at night, and how she used to love sitting beneath the window during the day, reaching out to grab the fine dust dancing in the rays of sunlight streaming in through the window. After a while, she'd draw back her hand and look inside—there was never anything there. Suddenly she had an overpowering desire to return to her cell, where she could talk with her cellmates for as long as they'd listen and enjoy a wonderful day with them. She climbed out of bed, got dressed, and hurriedly opened the door.

She was so surprised by what she saw she didn't know what to do: Jiang Hong, Xu Zifang, Chen Dehao, the woman who had come from so far away, Huang Li . . . all the women from Team One were there holding thermos boxes and plastic bags, standing quietly outside the window. When they saw her open the door, they rushed into the room, vying with one another to talk to her. "Do you know how long we've been waiting for you to open the door? Here, Group Leader Liu made these wontons for you. They're still hot!"

"They're filled with hawthorn paste. We're having a party, and the two of you are invited!"

As though she were waking from a dream, Li Zhenzi felt a surge of warmth coursing through her body. She reached out for Huang Li's hand and rubbed it. "How did you get here? Did you have a nice New Year's Eve at home? Was your old man there?"

"It was wonderful," Jiang Hong answered for the old woman. "Her old man had a change of heart! They went to a fish pond and she brought two huge fish back with her." Jiang Hong held out her hands to show how big the fish were, moving them in and out so much it made everyone laugh.

"I haven't forgotten that meal you made for me," Huang Li said with a smile.

"Your medical problem didn't come back, did it?" Jiang Hong quickly changed the subject out of an aversion to talking about anything from her past.

"That's enough chitchat," Xu Zifang said as she opened the thermos box in her hand. "The wontons are getting cold. Let her eat something first." She poured out two bowlfuls of steaming wontons and placed them in front of Li Zhenzi.

Jiang Hong dumped the sweet-rice dumplings out of a plastic bag onto a plate.

As though it were all planned, the women looked at her without asking where Shi Li had gone. They urged her to eat the wontons and the dumplings. Li Zhenzi was deeply touched. By not asking, they showed that they understood. Maybe the lifelong trials of being a woman had made suffering commonplace to them.

Li Zhenzi picked up a bowl of wontons and lowered her head as she forced back the tears. After all these years she had lost the feminine habit of crying, but over the past couple of days, tears had been her constant companion. She shut her eyes tightly and gobbled down a bowlful of wontons and the dumplings as though celebrating a victory, swallowing her troubles with each bite. When she was finished, she put down the bowl, stood up, and said to her friends, "Okay, let's go back to the cellblock and celebrate New Year's with the others."

"Let's go!" they echoed her.

"Let's go around the eastern yard," one of them recommended. "On my way over, a bunch of kids were setting off firecrackers there."

"Good idea! Let's go!" They noisily left the guesthouse and headed toward the eastern yard.

The air was filled with tiny, delicate snowflakes, falling with carefree self-assurance on the empty yard.

The women held hands as they walked across the snow-covered ground, their shoes making loud crunching sounds.

When Li Zhenzi saw the children having a snowball fight in their colorful new clothes, she raised her head and gazed up at the white sky. "It's wonderful!" she exclaimed emotionally.

"Happy New Year, Aunties! Here, have some sugary white New Year's cakes!" a boy in a red cap shouted. Snowballs arched through the air and landed on the prisoners' heads and bodies. They stood there like dummies, just watching the snowballs smash against them, sending powdery snow flying. After the first barrage the children stopped and stared at the snow-splattered figures in front of them, growing suddenly fearful. One or two had already retreated a few steps.

"Attack! Why don't we attack?" Jiang Hong's voice broke the silence. She scooped up a handful of snow and threw it at the children.

"Attack!" Her fellow prisoners, having snapped out of their confusion, rushed forward, shouting and scooping up ammunition. The children were quickly routed. Caught up in the frenzied joy of battle, some of the women grabbed the children and tossed them around, some picked them up and kissed them, some held on to them and rolled in the snow.

The children screamed in fright and fought to run away. Huang Li alone knelt in the snow in the middle of the yard, like a snowman, covered with snow and completely motionless.

145

AI BEI is a native of Beijing. After practicing medicine in a provincial hospital, she became a full-time writer. She has published over two dozen stories and novellas in major Chinese literary journals. In January 1989, Ai Bei arrived in the United States on an exchange visit sponsored by the United States Information Agency, where she attended a gathering of American writers. Stirred by the Tiananmen Incident of June 4th, she spoke over the Voice of America and university television stations and signed petitions protesting government actions. As a result, her wages in China were suspended by the government and she was ordered to return to China to be disciplined. She has taken up temporary residence in the United States, where she is traveling and writing.